C000128345

TouchPoints

gift edition

Books in the
TOUCHPOINTS™
Series

CP270

TouchPoints™
gift edition

TYNDALE HOUSE PUBLISHERS, INC.
CAROL STREAM, ILLINOIS

Visit Tyndale online at www.tyndale.com.

TYNDALE, Tyndale's quill logo, *New Living Translation*, NLT, and the New Living Translation logo are registered trademarks of Tyndale House Publishers, Inc. *TouchPoints* is a trademark of Tyndale House Publishers, Inc.

TouchPoints—Gift Edition

Previously published under ISBN 0-8423-7094-3.

Designed by Jackie L. Nuñez

ISBN 978-1-4143-3879-8

Printed in China

17 16 15 14 13 12 11
 7   6   5   4   3   2   1

CONTENTS

ABANDONMENT

Does my suffering mean that God has abandoned me?

1 SAMUEL 12:22 | *The LORD will not abandon his people.*

PSALM 9:10 | *Those who know your name trust in you, for you, O LORD, do not abandon those who search for you.*

1 PETER 5:10 | *In his kindness God called you to share in his eternal glory by means of Christ Jesus. So after you have suffered a little while, he will restore, support, and strengthen you, and he will place you on a firm foundation.*

Suffering does not mean God has left you. In fact, it is through suffering that you can experience God's comfort more than ever.

Does God promise to be with me at certain times but not at others?

MATTHEW 28:18, 20 | *Jesus came and told his disciples, . . . "Be sure of this: I am with you always, even to the end of the age."*

JOHN 14:16 | *[Jesus said,] "I will ask the Father, and he will give you another Advocate, who will never leave you."*

HEBREWS 13:5 | *Be satisfied with what you have. For God has said, "I will never fail you. I will never abandon you."*

God promises to be present with you, in you, and beside you in all circumstances.

Are there things I should abandon, even in these days of tolerance?

JOB 28:28 | *This is what [God] says to all humanity: "The fear of the Lord is true wisdom; to forsake evil is real understanding."*

EPHESIANS 4:31 | *Get rid of all bitterness, rage, anger, harsh words, and slander, as well as all types of evil behavior.*

Persistent sin will cause you to abandon God. Persistently obeying God will cause you to abandon much sin, which is important even in these days of tolerance.

Promise from God HEBREWS 13:5 | *I will never fail you. I will never abandon you.*

ACCEPTANCE

What if people have committed terrible sin? Should I still accept them?

ROMANS 8:39 | *Nothing . . . will ever be able to separate us from the love of God that is revealed in Christ Jesus our Lord.*

ROMANS 15:7 | *Accept each other just as Christ has accepted you so that God will be given glory.*

Nothing can separate a person from God's love. In the same way, you should always love others, no matter how great their sin. This does not mean that you accept or condone their sinful actions or ignore the appropriate discipline but that you view and accept them as unique and special creations of God. It is only through love that you bring sinful people back into fellowship with God and others.

I feel so unworthy—does God really accept me?

GENESIS 1:27 | *God created human beings in his own image. In the image of God he created them; male and female he created them.*

ROMANS 5:8 | *God showed his great love for us by sending Christ to die for us while we were still sinners.*

EPHESIANS 1:4-5 | *Even before he made the world, God loved us and chose us in Christ to be holy and without fault in his eyes. God decided in advance to adopt us into his own family by bringing us to himself through Jesus Christ. This is what he wanted to do, and it gave him great pleasure.*

You are accepted by God because he made you and created you in his image. Nothing you can do will cause God to love you more because he loves you completely. And nothing you do can cause God to love you less. In fact, God accepts you and loves you so much that he sent his own Son to die for you, to take on himself the punishment for sin you deserve. He died in your place so you can be accepted into eternity with him.

What should I never accept?

2 CHRONICLES 34:3-4 | *During the eighth year of his reign, while he was still young, Josiah began to seek the God of his ancestor David. . . . He ordered that the altars of Baal be demolished and that the incense altars which stood above them be broken down.*

ROMANS 6:12 | *Do not let sin control the way you live; do not give in to sinful desires.*

Never accept or tolerate sin in your life. Never feel satisfied that you sin less than someone else. Everyone has a sinful nature, and everyone has certain sins to which he or she is particularly vulnerable. If you leave sins unchecked, no matter how small, they will begin to grow and spread like malignant tumors, affecting all you think and do.

Promise from God ROMANS 15:7 | *Accept each other just as Christ has accepted you so that God will be given glory.*

ACCOUNTABILITY

How do I become more accountable?

PSALM 1:1 | *Oh, the joys of those who do not follow the advice of the wicked.*

PROVERBS 12:15 | *Fools think their own way is right, but the wise listen to others.*

To become more accountable, follow God's commands as outlined in his Word, the Bible. Part of being accountable is being a good listener and observer. You can learn much about your own behavior by observing others and listening to wise friends whom you respect. And choose wise friends to whom you can freely give an account of yourself.

What happens when there is no accountability?

GENESIS 16:6 | *Abram replied, "Look, she is your servant, so deal with her as you see fit." Then Sarai treated Hagar so harshly that she finally ran away.*

JUDGES 17:6 | *The people did whatever seemed right in their own eyes.*

Left unaccountable, people will always lean toward sin, the consequences of which eventually hurt them and others and pull them away from God. This could happen to you, as well.

How can I choose the right people to hold me accountable?

1 KINGS 12:8, 10-11 | *Rehoboam rejected the advice of the older men and instead asked the opinion of the young men who had grown up with him. . . . The young men replied, "This is what you should tell those complainers: . . . 'Yes, my father laid heavy burdens on you, but I'm going to make them even heavier! My father beat you with whips, but I will beat you with scorpions!'"*

Friends are not always the best advisers, especially if their counsel is not consistent with God's Word.

1 CORINTHIANS 12:8 | *To one person the Spirit gives the ability to give wise advice; to another the same Spirit gives a message of special knowledge.*

Choose people who are especially wise and godly, who will not hesitate to help you see when you need to realign yourself with God.

PROVERBS 13:17 | *An unreliable messenger stumbles into trouble, but a reliable messenger brings healing.*

Reliability in telling the truth is critical in those holding you accountable.

How can I hold someone else accountable effectively?

TITUS 1:7-9 | *An elder . . . must not be arrogant or quicktempered; he must not be . . . dishonest with money. . . . He must love what is good. He must live wisely and be just. He must live a devout and disciplined life. He must have a strong belief in the trustworthy message he was taught; then he will be able to encourage others with wholesome teaching and show those who oppose it where they are wrong.*

Before you can help others be accountable, you must not only know God's commands but consistently obey them and always work to develop good judgment yourself. If you are going to minister to others by holding them accountable, you must be wise, honest, godly, trustworthy, and kind.

Promise from God PSALM 119:9 | *How can a . . . person stay pure? By obeying your word.*

ADVERSITY

Is God listening when I cry out because of my troubles? Does he really hear, and does he care?

PSALM 18:6 | *In my distress I cried out to the LORD; yes, I prayed to my God for help. He heard me from his sanctuary; my cry to him reached his ears.*

MATTHEW 11:28 | *Jesus said, "Come to me, all of you who are weary and carry heavy burdens, and I will give you rest."*

God's hotline is always open. There is never a busy signal, and he is never too preoccupied with anything—even managing the universe—to listen to your every need. God has both a listening ear and a caring heart.

Will being faithful to God spare me from adversity?

DANIEL 3:16-20 | *Shadrach, Meshach, and Abednego replied, "O Nebuchadnezzar, we do not need to defend ourselves before you. If we are thrown into the blazing furnace, the God whom we serve is able to save us. . . . But even if he doesn't, we want to make it clear . . . that we will never serve your gods or worship the gold statue you have set up." Nebuchadnezzar was so furious . . . he commanded that the furnace be heated seven times hotter than usual. Then he ordered some of the strongest men of his army to bind Shadrach, Meshach, and Abednego and throw them into the blazing furnace.*

ACTS 5:17-18 | *The high priest and his officials, who were Sadducees, were filled with jealousy. They arrested the apostles and put them in the public jail.*

The lives of believers in both the Old and New Testaments testify that being faithful to God does not eliminate adversity. When you believe in Jesus, Satan becomes your enemy. He will try to stop you from following God by sending you all kinds of adversity. Recognize that it may be a sign that you are being faithful to God.

NAHUM 1:7 | *The LORD is good, a strong refuge when trouble comes. He is close to those who trust in him.*

In most cases, the Bible doesn't say *if* trouble will come, but *when* trouble comes. No one has lived his or her life without some adversity.

PSALM 27:5, 7-8 | *He will conceal me . . . when troubles come; he will hide me in his sanctuary. He will place me out of reach on a high rock. . . . Hear me as I pray, O LORD. Be merciful and answer me! My heart has heard you say, "Come and talk with me." And my heart responds, "LORD, I am coming."*

Sometimes God does rescue you from adversity because of your faithfulness.

Is there any way I can avoid trouble and adversity?

JAMES 1:2-3 | *When troubles come your way, consider it an opportunity for great joy. For you know that when your faith is tested, your endurance has a chance to grow.*

Avoiding adversity may not be best for you. Though hard times may bruise you, they also can build you up and strengthen your faith.

PROVERBS 14:16 | *The wise are cautious and avoid danger; fools plunge ahead with reckless confidence.*

ROMANS 13:14 | *Clothe yourself with the presence of the Lord Jesus Christ. And don't let yourself think about ways to indulge your evil desires.*

The consequences of sin often bring unneeded adversity into your life. By obeying God's Word, you can avoid many kinds of adversity you might otherwise inflict on yourself.

PROVERBS 17:20 | *The crooked heart will not prosper; the lying tongue tumbles into trouble.*

PROVERBS 21:23 | *Watch your tongue and keep your mouth shut, and you will stay out of trouble.*

Controlling your tongue can help you avoid adversity. Many times trouble can be avoided by using words wisely.

PROVERBS 11:14 | *There is safety in having many advisers.*

Following advice from godly people will help you avoid trouble.

Promise from God PSALM 46:1 | *God is our refuge and strength, always ready to help in times of trouble.*

AMBITION

When is ambition good?

PSALM 119:1-2 | *Joyful are people of integrity, who follow the instructions of the LORD. Joyful are those who obey his laws and search for him with all their hearts.*

The purest ambition of all is to pursue knowing God and to try to do what he asks.

1 THESSALONIANS 4:11-12 | *Make it your goal to live a quiet life, minding your own business and working with your hands, just as we instructed you before. Then people who are not Christians will respect the way you live.*

Ambition is good when it is directed at improving the quality of your character, not at promoting your accomplishments.

ROMANS 15:20 | *[Paul said,] "My ambition has always been to preach the Good News where the name of Christ has never been heard."*

A great ambition is to tell others about Jesus wherever you go, as Paul did.

When does ambition become destructive or sinful? What is the danger of ambition?

GENESIS 11:4 | *[The people] said, "Come, let's build a great city for ourselves with a tower that reaches into the sky. This will make us famous and keep us from being scattered all over the world."*

Ambition becomes wrong when its goal is to bring glory to yourself instead of the God who gave you your talents and abilities.

MATTHEW 4:9 | *"I will give it all to you," [the devil] said, "if you will kneel down and worship me."*

Ambition can become destructive if Satan uses it to lure you away from God. You can test your ambition by asking if what you want to do will lead you closer to or further away from God. If you're not sure, then it is likely leading you away from him.

MARK 10:35-37, 41 | *James and John, the sons of Zebedee, came over and spoke to [Jesus]. "Teacher," they said, "we want you to do us a favor." "What is your request?" he asked. They replied, "When you sit on your glorious throne, we want to sit in places of honor next to you, one on your right and the other on your left."... When the ten other disciples heard what James and John had asked, they were indignant.*

Selfish ambition can twist your friendships and service to God into trivial competitiveness.

How can I use ambition to glorify God?

1 KINGS 8:58 | *May [the Lord] give us the desire to do his will in everything and to obey all the commands, decrees, and regulations that he gave our ancestors.*

PSALM 73:25 | *Whom have I in heaven but you? I desire you more than anything on earth.*

Your motives signal whether your actions are based on selfish ambition or on godly ambition. When your greatest desire is to do God's will, when loving and serving others is your greatest goal, and when you focus every day on praising and worshiping God, then you are pursuing the godly ambition of glorifying him.

Promise from God PSALM 119:1-2 | *Joyful are people of integrity, who follow the instructions of the LORD. Joyful are those who obey his laws and search for him with all their hearts.*

ANGER

Why do I get angry?

GENESIS 4:4-5 | *The LORD accepted Abel and his gift, but he did not accept Cain and his gift. This made Cain very angry, and he looked dejected.*

NUMBERS 22:29 | *"You have made me look like a fool!" Balaam shouted.*

ESTHER 3:5 | *When Haman saw that Mordecai would not bow down or show him respect, he was filled with rage.*

Anger is often a reaction to your pride being hurt. It is common to feel angry when you have been confronted about your own sinful actions, because you don't want others to think you have done something wrong.

1 SAMUEL 18:8 | *Saul [became] very angry. "What's this?" he said. "They credit David with ten thousands and me with only thousands. Next they'll be making him their king!"*

Anger is often a reaction of jealousy to what others have or to what others have accomplished.

What are the effects of anger?

GENESIS 27:41-43 | *Esau hated Jacob because their father had given Jacob the blessing. And Esau began to scheme: ". . . I will kill my brother, Jacob." But Rebekah heard about Esau's plans. So she sent for Jacob and told him, "Listen, Esau is . . . plotting to kill you. . . . Flee to my brother, Laban, in Haran."*

Anger isolates you from others.

PSALM 37:8 | *Stop being angry! . . . Do not lose your temper— it only leads to harm.*

JAMES 1:19-20 | *You must all be quick to listen, slow to speak, and slow to get angry. Human anger does not produce the righteousness God desires.*

Anger produces ungodliness and evil motives in you.

1 SAMUEL 20:30-31 | *Saul boiled with rage at Jonathan. . . . "As long as that son of Jesse is alive, you'll never be king. Now go and get him so I can kill him!"*

Anger blinds you to what is really good and right. In its strongest form, anger can lead to murder.

PROVERBS 15:1 | *A gentle answer deflects anger, but harsh words make tempers flare.*

Anger leads to conflict and arguments.

What makes God angry?

EPHESIANS 2:2-3 | *You used to live in sin, just like the rest of the world, obeying the devil. . . . He is the spirit at work in the hearts of those who refuse to obey God. All of us used to live that way, following the passionate desires and inclinations of our sinful nature. By our very nature we were subject to God's anger, just like everyone else.*

God cannot wink at or tolerate sin, for sin is a deliberate violation of his righteousness and makes him angry.

JUDGES 2:13-14 | *They abandoned the LORD. . . . This made the LORD burn with anger.*

When people deliberately turn away from God and abandon him, it angers God because he created them for relationship.

MALACHI 3:5 | *"At that time I will put you on trial. . . . I will speak against those who cheat employees of their wages, who oppress widows and orphans, or who deprive the foreigners living among you of justice, for these people do not fear me," says the LORD of Heaven's Armies.*

God gets angry when people neglect or abuse the unfortunate and those in need.

Is God angry with me?

PSALM 145:8 | *The LORD is merciful and compassionate, slow to get angry and filled with unfailing love.*

1 THESSALONIANS 5:9 | *God chose to save us through our Lord Jesus Christ, not to pour out his anger on us.*

The Bible promises that God is kind and merciful and always ready to receive you, and all his children, with love. The "always-angry God" is one of the worst caricatures ever attributed to God. His anger toward us is conveyed with gentle discipline and is an expression of his love in action.

We all get angry at times, so what should I do about it?

EPHESIANS 4:26-27 | *"Don't sin by letting anger control you." Don't let the sun go down while you are still angry, for anger gives a foothold to the devil.*

Stay under the control of the Holy Spirit through prayer, and try to resolve your anger quickly. Like a skunk in the house, anger permeates all aspects of your life. Don't encourage anger to stay by feeding it. Get rid of it as soon as possible.

EPHESIANS 6:4 | *Do not provoke your children to anger by the way you treat them.*

Avoid punishing your children in the heat of anger.

MATTHEW 5:21-22, 24 | *[Jesus said,] "You have heard that our ancestors were told, 'You must not murder.'. . . But I say, if you are even angry with someone, you are subject to judgment! . . . Go and be reconciled to that person."*

JAMES 3:5 | *The tongue is a small thing that makes grand speeches. But a tiny spark can set a great forest on fire.*

Avoid "speaking your mind" when you are angry. You are bound to say something you will regret. Calmly confront those with whom you are angry in order to restore your relationship.

1 SAMUEL 19:9-10 | *As David played his harp, Saul hurled his spear at David. But David dodged out of the way, and leaving the spear stuck in the wall, he fled and escaped into the night.*

Avoid acting on impulse in the heat of anger. You are bound to do something you will regret.

1 CORINTHIANS 13:5 | *[Love] is not irritable, and it keeps no record of being wronged.*

Love is the mightiest weapon in overcoming anger.

Promise from God PSALM 103:8 | *The LORD is compassionate and merciful, slow to get angry and filled with unfailing love.*

ASSUMPTIONS

What are some assumptions I should avoid?

JOHN 14:6 | *Jesus [said], "I am the way, the truth, and the life. No one can come to the Father except through me."*

Don't just assume you will go to heaven. The Bible says the only way to heaven is by accepting Jesus Christ as Savior and Lord.

ROMANS 5:8-9, 11 | *God showed his great love for us by sending Christ to die for us while we were still sinners. And since we have been made right in God's sight by the blood of Christ, he will certainly save us from God's condemnation. . . . So now we can rejoice in our wonderful new relationship with God because our Lord Jesus Christ has made us friends of God.*

Don't assume God doesn't care, for evidence shows he clearly does.

JUDGES 6:13-14 | *"Sir," Gideon replied, "if the LORD is with us, why has all this happened to us? And where are all the miracles our ancestors told us about? Didn't they say, 'The LORD brought us up out of Egypt'? But now the LORD has abandoned us and handed us over to the Midianites." Then the LORD turned to him and said, "Go with the strength you have, and rescue Israel from the Midianites. I am sending you!"*

Don't assume God won't help you or doesn't want to help you, for he has already done so in more ways than you know, and he will continue to do so. And don't assume you know better than God the best way through your problems.

ACTS 9:13, 15 | *"Lord," exclaimed Ananias, "I've heard many people talk about the terrible things this man has done to the believers in Jerusalem!" . . . But the Lord said, "Go, for Saul is my chosen instrument to take my message to the Gentiles and to kings, as well as to the people of Israel."*

Don't assume people can't change; you may miss out when they want to give their best to you. Like Paul (previously known as Saul), even the worst sinner can become a great Christian leader.

JOHN 3:8 | *Just as you can hear the wind but can't tell where it comes from or where it is going, so you can't explain how people are born of the Spirit.*

ACTS 16:27-30 | *The jailer woke up to see the prison doors wide open. He assumed the prisoners had escaped, so he drew his sword to kill himself. But Paul shouted to him, "Stop! Don't kill yourself! We are all here!" The jailer called for lights and ran to the dungeon and fell down trembling before Paul and Silas. Then he brought them out and asked, "Sirs, what must I do to be saved?"*

Don't assume that someone won't respond to the gospel. In God's hands, people can be transformed into godly heroes.

Promise from God 1 CORINTHIANS 4:5 | *Don't make judgments about anyone ahead of time—before the Lord returns. For he will bring our darkest secrets to light and will reveal our private motives. Then God will give to each one whatever praise is due.*

BELONGING

Why is it important to feel that I belong somewhere—to a family, a spouse, a church?

PSALM 73:23-24 | *I still belong to you; you hold my right hand. You guide me with your counsel, leading me to a glorious destiny.*

ROMANS 1:6 | *You are included among those . . . who have been called to belong to Jesus Christ.*

We all need a sense of belonging, for in belonging are security and acceptance. And when you belong to God, that security and acceptance can never be taken away— it lasts for eternity.

What happens when I belong to God?

DEUTERONOMY 28:10 | *All the nations of the world will see that you are a people claimed by the LORD, and they will stand in awe.*

God has claimed you.

ISAIAH 26:19 | *Those who die in the LORD will live; their bodies will rise again! Those who sleep in the earth will rise up and sing for joy! For your life-giving light will fall like dew on your people in the place of the dead!*

You are assured of eternal life.

JOHN 15:12-13, 15 | *[Jesus said,] "Love each other in the same way I have loved you. There is no greater love than to lay down one's life for one's friends. . . . I no longer call you slaves, because a master doesn't confide in his slaves. Now you are my friends."*

You more fully understand how to love others.

How can I be sure I belong to God?

1 JOHN 2:3-5 | *We can be sure that we know him if we obey his commandments. If someone claims, "I know God," but doesn't obey God's commandments, that person is a liar and is not living in the truth. But those who obey God's word truly show how completely they love him. That is how we know we are living in him.*

1 JOHN 3:10 | *We can tell who are children of God and who are children of the devil. Anyone who does not live righteously and does not love other believers does not belong to God.*

Obedience to God is a reflection of love for him and belief in him. Since you are human, you will not obey God perfectly all the time. But what God looks for is a desire to please and obey him, as well as a commitment to make your best effort to do so every day.

Promise from God LEVITICUS 26:12 | *I will walk among you; I will be your God, and you will be my people.*

BIBLE

Can I truly trust the Bible as God's Word?

PSALM 18:30 | *God's way is perfect. All the LORD's promises prove true.*

2 TIMOTHY 3:16 | *All Scripture is inspired by God and is useful to teach us what is true and to make us realize what is wrong in our lives. It corrects us when we are wrong and teaches us to do what is right.*

2 PETER 1:20-21 | *No prophecy in Scripture ever came from the prophet's own understanding, or from human initiative. No, those prophets were moved by the Holy Spirit, and they spoke from God.*

The Bible has stood the test of time more than any other document in human history. It has been faithfully preserved because it is God's very words to us, and he will not let them disappear from the face of the earth or be altered by human hands.

How often should I read the Bible?

DEUTERONOMY 17:19 | *[The king] must always keep [God's written instruction] with him and read it daily as long as he lives. That way he will learn to fear the LORD his God by obeying all the terms of these instructions and decrees.*

JOSHUA 1:8 | *Study this Book of Instruction continually. Meditate on it day and night so you will be sure to obey everything written in it. Only then will you prosper and succeed in all you do.*

The Bible is for regular reading and meditation in order to learn about God and communicate with him. If at all possible, this should be done daily. When God says "continually" study his Word, he doesn't mean reading the Bible just when you get around to it.

Why is it so important to read the Bible?

JEREMIAH 15:16 | *When I discovered your words, I devoured them. They are my joy and my heart's delight, for I bear your name, O LORD God of Heaven's Armies.*

God's Word shapes your heart, mind, and soul. It brings true joy and purpose to life. And it inspires you to live a life that reflects God's character and leaves a lasting spiritual legacy.

PSALM 119:9 | *How can a young person stay pure? By obeying your word.*

PSALM 119:11 | *I have hidden your word in my heart, that I might not sin against you.*

Reading the Bible is the way to know how to live a holy life before God.

ACTS 17:11 | *The people of Berea were more open-minded than those in Thessalonica, and they listened eagerly to Paul's message. They searched the Scriptures day after day to see if Paul and Silas were teaching the truth.*

Reading the Bible helps you recognize true and false teaching.

DEUTERONOMY 17:20 | *Regular reading will prevent him from becoming proud and acting as if he is above his fellow citizens.*

Reading the Bible helps you keep a right attitude toward God and others.

PSALM 119:105 | *Your word is a lamp to guide my feet and a light for my path.*

Reading the Bible guides you in daily living.

PSALM 119:24 | *Your laws please me; they give me wise advice.*

PROVERBS 6:22 | *When you walk, their counsel will lead you. When you sleep, they will protect you. When you wake up, they will advise you.*

Reading the Bible provides good counsel for your problems.

PSALM 119:43 | *Your regulations are my only hope.*

PSALM 119:52 | *I meditate on your age-old regulations; O LORD, they comfort me.*

Reading the Bible gives great comfort and hope.

Promise from God LUKE 11:28 | *Blessed are all who hear the word of God and put it into practice.*

BITTERNESS

How do I become bitter?

GENESIS 27:41 | *From that time on, Esau hated Jacob because their father had given Jacob the blessing. And Esau began to scheme.*

ESTHER 5:9 | *Haman was a happy man as he left the banquet! But when he saw Mordecai sitting at the palace gate, not standing up or trembling nervously before him, Haman became furious.*

Bitterness grows as you allow anger and then hatred to control you.

2 SAMUEL 2:26 | *Abner shouted down to Joab, "Must we always be killing each other? Don't you realize that bitterness is the*

only result? When will you call off your men from chasing their Israelite brothers?"

Bitterness grows the more you retaliate for wrongs done against you.

2 CORINTHIANS 2:7 | *It is time to forgive and comfort him. Otherwise he may be overcome by discouragement.*

COLOSSIANS 3:13 | *Make allowance for each other's faults, and forgive anyone who offends you. Remember, the Lord forgave you, so you must forgive others.*

Bitterness comes when others hurt you and you refuse to forgive. Never stop forgiving and forgetting. Remember that God has forgiven you despite your continual tendency to sin.

HEBREWS 12:15 | *Look after each other so that none of you fails to receive the grace of God. Watch out that no poisonous root of bitterness grows up to trouble you, corrupting many.*

Bitterness comes when you forget God's grace, which is showered on you each day.

How do I deal with my bitterness toward others?

MARK 11:25 | *When you are praying, first forgive anyone you are holding a grudge against, so that your Father in heaven will forgive your sins, too.*

EPHESIANS 4:31-32 | *Get rid of all bitterness. . . . Instead, be kind to each other, tenderhearted, forgiving one another, just as God through Christ has forgiven you.*

Forgiveness is the antidote to bitterness. It lifts burdens, cancels debts, and frees you from the chains of unresolved anger.

PHILIPPIANS 1:12, 14 | *[Paul said,] "I want you to know, my dear brothers and sisters, that everything that has happened to me here has helped to spread the Good News. . . . Because of my imprisonment, most of the believers here have gained confidence and boldly speak God's message without fear."*

Paul was traveling the world spreading the good news about Jesus. Then he was thrown into prison for sharing his faith! That could have made him bitter. Instead, he was joyful because he saw it as an opportunity. He knew that God takes even the worst situations and brings good out of them. While in prison, Paul wrote many of the New Testament letters, which have brought countless millions to faith in Jesus.

Promise from God ISAIAH 26:3 | *You will keep in perfect peace all who trust in you, all whose thoughts are fixed on you!*

BLESSINGS

How can I receive God's blessings?

EPHESIANS 1:3 | *All praise to God, the Father of our Lord Jesus Christ, who has blessed us with every spiritual blessing in the heavenly realms because we are united with Christ.*

When you belong to Christ, you understand that all you are and all you have are gifts from him, to be used by him to bless others. When you truly desire to serve God, you will find yourself in the middle of a rushing stream of God's blessings, to be used to refresh others.

DEUTERONOMY 1:35-36 | *Not one of you from this wicked generation will live to see the good land I swore to give your ancestors, except Caleb. . . . He will see this land because he has followed the LORD completely.*

Throughout the Bible, you find a simple but profound principle: Obeying God brings blessings, and disobeying God brings misfortune. Be careful not to think of God's blessings only in terms of material possessions—the greatest blessings are far more valuable than money or things. They come in the form of joy, family, relationships, peace of heart, spiritual gifts, and the confidence of eternal life.

How has God promised to bless his people?

NUMBERS 6:24-26 | *May the LORD bless you and protect you. May the LORD smile on you and be gracious to you. May the LORD show you his favor and give you his peace.*

Like the constant movement of the ocean, God's blessings are constant, whether you are aware of them or not. Scripture is full of blessings God gives to those who love him, including his presence, his grace, and his peace.

EPHESIANS 1:2, 13-14 | *May God our Father and the Lord Jesus Christ give you grace and peace. . . . When you believed in Christ, he identified you as his own by giving you the Holy Spirit, whom he promised long ago. The Spirit is God's guarantee that he will give us the inheritance he promised and that he has purchased us to be his own people.*

Jesus Christ blesses you with forgiveness and redemption. God the Father blesses you with the assurance that you are loved and of infinite worth. The Holy Spirit blesses you with fellowship and the continuous presence of God.

How can I be a blessing to others?

2 CORINTHIANS 2:14 | *Thank God! He has made us his captives and continues to lead us along in Christ's triumphal procession. Now he uses us to spread the knowledge of Christ everywhere, like a sweet perfume.*

As you share the blessings God has poured on you, you bless others as well. Encouraging others with God's good news is one of the most rewarding of his blessings.

Should I bless my enemies?

ROMANS 12:14 | *Bless those who persecute you. Don't curse them; pray that God will bless them.*

Jesus introduced a revolutionary new idea—blessing and forgiving enemies. The natural response is revenge for enemies. Prayer for your enemies is a severe test of your devotion to Christ. Which is the greater blessing: to win over your enemies or to continue fighting with them?

Promise from God GALATIANS 6:9 | *Let's not get tired of doing what is good. At just the right time we will reap a harvest of blessing if we don't give up.*

BOREDOM

Isn't being a Christian boring?

JOHN 15:11 | *I have told you these things so that you will be filled with my joy. Yes, your joy will overflow!*

HEBREWS 6:11-12 | *Our great desire is that you will keep on loving others as long as life lasts, in order to make certain that what you hope for will come true. Then you will not become spiritually dull and indifferent. Instead, you will follow the example of those who are going to inherit God's promises because of their faith and endurance.*

Those who grasp what the Christian life is all about find it full and exciting. When you realize that God wants to work through you to accomplish some of his work in the world, you will be amazed to see the great things he will do. Focus on using and developing your God-given gifts, and your life will be continually exciting.

Isn't a sinful way of life more exciting?

JEREMIAH 2:25 | *When will you stop running? When will you stop panting after other gods?*

Chasing other "gods" is a tiring business—one pursuit after another ends with disappointment and dissatisfaction. Sin has a debilitating sameness at its core. God alone truly satisfies.

Promise from God JOHN 15:11 | *I have told you these things so that you will be filled with my joy. Yes, your joy will overflow!*

BROKENNESS

Why is brokenness so important?

PSALM 34:18 | *The LORD is close to the brokenhearted; he rescues those whose spirits are crushed.*

PSALM 147:3 | *He heals the brokenhearted and bandages their wounds.*

Brokenness is the awareness of our full dependence on God. It signifies the breaking of our pride and self-sufficiency. Brokenness comes most often through circumstances that overwhelm us or through sin that seduces us. Those who are open about their brokenness—as were Moses, David, Jesus, and Paul—often have greater influence over others because of that.

PSALM 51:17 | *The sacrifice you desire is a broken spirit. You will not reject a broken and repentant heart, O God.*

God promises to draw close to you when you are broken-hearted about sin in your life. When you turn to God in brokenness over your sin, he begins to heal and restore you.

JOB 2:8-10 | *Job scraped his skin with a piece of broken pottery as he sat among the ashes. His wife said to him, "Are you still trying to maintain your integrity? Curse God and die." But Job replied, ". . . Should we accept only good things from the hand of God and never anything bad?" So in all this, Job said nothing wrong.*

The alternative to brokenness before God is bitterness, which leads to dissatisfaction and a general irritation with life. Bitterness never allows God the opportunity to heal you, for a bitter person looks inward, not upward. Job looked upward.

ISAIAH 66:2 | *[The Lord says,] "I will bless those who have humble and contrite hearts, who tremble at my word."*

Humility is a form of brokenness, the realization that you cannot fix nor can you control your needs. Acknowledging your dependence on God allows him to help you with all your needs.

Promise from God PSALM 34:18 | *The LORD is close to the brokenhearted; he rescues those whose spirits are crushed.*

CALL OF GOD

How do I know what my calling from God is?

PSALM 119:105 | *Your word is a lamp to guide my feet and a light for my path.*

The first step in knowing your calling is to get to know God better by reading his Word. As God communicates to you through the Bible, he will show you what to do and where he wants you to go.

DANIEL 1:17 | *God gave these four young men an unusual aptitude for understanding every aspect of literature and wisdom. And God gave Daniel the special ability to interpret the meanings of visions and dreams.*

God has given every individual special aptitudes and abilities. These provide the biggest clue to what God wants you to do. In the meantime, develop those special abilities and begin to use them. In God's timing, you will see what he wants you to do.

ACTS 20:24 | *[Paul said,] "My life is worth nothing to me unless I use it for finishing the work assigned me by the Lord Jesus."*

When God gives you a specific calling, it fills your thoughts and energies so that you have a longing to pursue it whole-heartedly.

ROMANS 12:2 | *Let God transform you into a new person by changing the way you think. Then you will learn to know God's will for you.*

When you let God transform you by the power of his Holy Spirit, he will literally begin to change the way you think so you will know what he wants you to do.

JEREMIAH 1:4-5 | *The LORD gave me this message: "I knew you before I formed you in your mother's womb. Before you were born I set you apart and appointed you as my prophet to the nations."*

God may call you to do a certain job or to accomplish a very specific task or ministry. When that happens, you will feel a very strong sense of leading from him. It's up to you to respond and walk through the door of opportunity he opens.

1 CORINTHIANS 12:4, 7 | *There are different kinds of spiritual gifts, but the same Spirit is the source of them all. . . . A spiritual gift is given to each of us so we can help each other.*

God gives each individual a spiritual gift (sometimes more than one!) and a special ministry in the church. You can use your gifts to help and encourage others and to bring glory to his name. These specific spiritual gifts help you fulfill the purpose for which God made you.

1 CORINTHIANS 10:31 | *Whatever you do, do it all for the glory of God.*

GALATIANS 5:14, 16 | *The whole law can be summed up in this one command: "Love your neighbor as yourself." . . . So I say, let the Holy Spirit guide your lives. Then you won't be doing what your sinful nature craves.*

The call to follow Jesus does not necessarily mean a call to a specific job or Christian ministry. Sometimes your call may simply be to obey God wherever you are right now.

Promise from God 1 THESSALONIANS 5:23-24 | *May the God of peace make you holy in every way, and may your whole spirit and soul and body be kept blameless until our Lord Jesus Christ comes again. God will make this happen, for he who calls you is faithful.*

CELEBRATION

Does God want me to celebrate? Is it okay?

DEUTERONOMY 16:10-11, 15 | *Celebrate the Festival of Harvest to honor the LORD your God. . . . This is a time to celebrate before the LORD your God. . . . Celebrate with your sons and daughters, . . . for it is he who blesses you with bountiful harvests and gives you success in all your work. This festival will be a time of great joy for all.*

2 SAMUEL 22:1-3 | *David sang this song to the LORD on the day the LORD rescued him from all his enemies . . . : "The LORD is my rock, my fortress, and my savior; my God is my rock, in whom I find protection. He is my shield, the power that saves me, and my place of safety. He is my refuge, my savior, the one who saves me from violence."*

Not only is God okay with celebration, he encourages it as a way for you to thank him for all he has done, to recall his acts of goodness, and to enjoy the company of others.

MATTHEW 25:23 | *The master said, "Well done, my good and faithful servant. You have been faithful in handling this small amount, so now I will give you many more responsibilities. Let's celebrate together!"*

Task-oriented individuals can sometimes neglect the opportunity to celebrate. The Bible teaches that celebration is both important and necessary. Celebration gives you the opportunity to savor the joy of work, to experience the satisfaction and rewards of accomplishment, and to enjoy the good things of creation. It creates a spirit of gratitude and renews your energy for the work that still must be done.

What causes God and the angels to celebrate?

MATTHEW 25:23 | *The master said, "Well done, my good and faithful servant. You have been faithful in handling this small amount, so now I will give you many more responsibilities. Let's celebrate together!"*

LUKE 15:10 | *There is joy in the presence of God's angels when even one sinner repents.*

God and the angels celebrate the salvation of the lost, the defeat of sin and evil, and the daily joys and successes of God's people.

ZEPHANIAH 3:17 | *The LORD your God . . . will take delight in you with gladness. . . . He will rejoice over you with joyful songs.*

God rejoices and celebrates when his people faithfully follow him and obey his commands.

Promise from God PSALM 5:11 | *Let all who take refuge in you rejoice; let them sing joyful praises forever. Spread your protection over them, that all who love your name may be filled with joy.*

CHANGE

With all the change in my life, how can I keep it all together?

LAMENTATIONS 5:19 | *LORD, you remain the same forever! Your throne continues from generation to generation.*

HEBREWS 1:12 | *You are always the same; you will live forever.*

The character of God is loving and trustworthy—and unchanging. This is good news, because no matter how much your life changes, no matter what new situations you face, you can always count on God's promise to care for, help, and guide you.

MARK 13:31 | *Heaven and earth will disappear, but my words will never disappear.*

The truths in the Bible apply to all people in all cultures over all time. As you face change, constantly turn to God's unchanging Word to give your life a rock-solid foundation and direction.

GENESIS 37:28; 41:39-41 | *When the Ishmaelites, who were Midianite traders, came by, Joseph's brothers pulled him out of the cistern and sold him to them for twenty pieces of silver. And the traders took him to Egypt. . . . Then Pharaoh said to Joseph, . . . "You will be in charge of my court, and all my people will take orders from you. Only I, sitting on my throne, will have a rank higher than yours. . . . I hereby put you in charge of the entire land of Egypt."*

ROMANS 8:28 | *We know that God causes everything to work together for the good of those who love God and are called according to his purpose for them.*

Sometimes change seems to be for the worse. When such change occurs, remember that traumatic, unpredictable, and unfair change never trumps God's will. No change occurs that he does not allow and that he cannot redeem.

I know there are things in my life I should change, but how?

ACTS 9:4-5 | *He fell to the ground and heard a voice saying to him, "Saul! Saul! Why are you persecuting me?" "Who are you, lord?" Saul asked. And the voice replied, "I am Jesus."*

Real change comes as the result of a personal encounter with Jesus Christ.

LUKE 19:8 | *Zacchaeus stood before the Lord and said, "I will give half my wealth to the poor, Lord, and if I have cheated people on their taxes, I will give them back four times as much!"*

God calls not only for a change of heart but for a change of behavior.

JOHN 8:10-11 | *[Jesus said,] "Where are your accusers? Didn't even one of them condemn you?" "No, Lord," she said. And Jesus said, "Neither do I. Go and sin no more."*

You do not change in order to receive God's approval; you change as you respond to God's love.

2 CORINTHIANS 5:17 | *Anyone who belongs to Christ has become a new person. The old life is gone; a new life has begun!*

PHILIPPIANS 1:6 | *God, who began the good work within you, will continue his work until it is finally finished on the day when Christ Jesus returns.*

A great work takes a long time to complete. Though you became a believer in a moment of faith, the process of transformation into being like Jesus takes a lifetime. While it may appear slow, God's work in you is relentless and certain and positive.

Promise from God ISAIAH 40:8 | *The grass withers and the flowers fade, but the word of our God stands forever.*

CHEATING

What does God think of cheating? Is it always wrong?

LEVITICUS 19:11 | *Do not deceive or cheat one another.*

PROVERBS 11:1 | *The LORD detests the use of dishonest scales, but he delights in accurate weights.*

If you want God's blessing, you must live by his standards of fairness and justice. Cheating is the opposite of honesty because the motives behind it are always to deceive someone else.

ROMANS 13:9-10 | *The commandments say, "You must not commit adultery. You must not murder. You must not steal. You must not covet." These—and other such commandments— are summed up in this one commandment: "Love your neighbor as yourself." Love does no wrong to others, so love fulfills the requirements of God's law.*

Cheating is evidence that you do not love or respect the person you cheated and that you are thinking only of yourself.

PSALM 101:7 | *I will not allow deceivers to serve in my house, and liars will not stay in my presence.*

When you cheat, you are actually cheating yourself of what God has planned for you.

Is some cheating worse than other cheating?

MARK 12:40 | *[The teachers of religious law] shamelessly cheat widows out of their property and then pretend to be pious by making long prayers in public. Because of this, they will be more severely punished.*

Sin is sin, but some sin receives greater punishment from God. Cheating those who are less fortunate and then covering it up by trying to make your actions look spiritual is a double sin: first, the sin of cheating and, second, the sin of pious deceit.

LUKE 16:10 | *If you are faithful in little things, you will be faithful in large ones. But if you are dishonest in little things, you won't be honest with greater responsibilities.*

Character is tested in the small choices you make. A little bit of cheating is cut out of the same piece of cloth as a lot of cheating. Just as a small drop of red dye colors a large glass of clear water, a small act of deception colors your character.

Promise from God PROVERBS 11:1 | *The LORD detests the use of dishonest scales, but he delights in accurate weights.*

COMFORT

When does God comfort me?

MATTHEW 5:4 | *God blesses those who mourn, for they will be comforted.*

When you grieve.

PSALM 145:14 | *The LORD helps the fallen and lifts those bent beneath their loads.*

When you are overwhelmed.

GENESIS 26:24 | *Do not be afraid, for I am with you and will bless you.*

When you are afraid.

MATTHEW 5:11 | *God blesses you when people mock you and persecute you and lie about you and say all sorts of evil things against you because you are my followers.*

When you are persecuted.

JOHN 16:33 | *Here on earth you will have many trials and sorrows. But take heart, because I have overcome the world.*

When you are suffering.

PSALM 138:3 | *As soon as I pray, you answer me; you encourage me by giving me strength.*

When you are weak and weary.

ROMANS 8:28 | *We know that God causes everything to work together for the good of those who love God and are called according to his purpose for them.*

When you worry about your future.

How does God comfort me?

PSALM 119:76 | *Let your unfailing love comfort me, just as you promised me, your servant.*

He loves you.

ROMANS 8:26 | *The Holy Spirit helps us in our weakness. For example, we don't know what God wants us to pray for. But the Holy Spirit prays for us with groanings that cannot be expressed in words.*

He prays for you.

PSALM 55:17 | *Morning, noon, and night I cry out in my distress, and the LORD hears my voice.*

He listens to you.

PSALM 94:19 | *When doubts filled my mind, your comfort gave me renewed hope and cheer.*

He gives you hope and joy.

PSALM 147:3 | *He heals the brokenhearted and bandages their wounds.*

He heals your broken heart.

How can I comfort others?

JOB 42:11 | *All his brothers, sisters, and former friends came and feasted with him in his home. And they consoled him and comforted him because of all the trials the LORD had brought against him.*

You can be with them in their time of need. Just being there speaks volumes about how much you care.

JOB 21:2 | *Listen closely to what I am saying. That's one consolation you can give me.*

You can be a good listener. It is usually more important for you to listen than to talk.

RUTH 2:13 | *"I hope I continue to please you, sir," she replied. "You have comforted me by speaking so kindly to me, even though I am not one of your workers."*

You can speak kind and encouraging words.

PHILEMON 1:7 | *[Paul said,] "Your love has given me much joy and comfort, my brother, for your kindness has often refreshed the hearts of God's people."*

You can comfort others with kind actions.

2 CORINTHIANS 1:3-4 | *All praise to God, the Father of our Lord Jesus Christ. God is our merciful Father and the source of all comfort. He comforts us in all our troubles so that we can*

comfort others. When they are troubled, we will be able to give them the same comfort God has given us.

Remember the ways God has comforted you, and model that same comfort to others. When you have experienced God's assuring love, his guiding wisdom, and his sustaining power, you are able to comfort others with understanding.

Promise from God PSALM 94:19 | *When doubts filled my mind, your comfort gave me renewed hope and cheer.*

COMMUNICATION

How does God communicate with me?

JEREMIAH 36:2 | *Get a scroll, and write down all my messages.*

2 TIMOTHY 3:16-17 | *All Scripture is inspired by God and is useful to teach us what is true and to make us realize what is wrong in our lives. It corrects us when we are wrong and teaches us to do what is right. God uses it to prepare and equip his people to do every good work.*

God communicates with you through his Word, the Bible. Read it daily to keep in touch with him.

JOHN 1:14 | *The Word became human and made his home among us. He was full of unfailing love and faithfulness. And we have seen his glory, the glory of the Father's one and only Son.*

HEBREWS 1:1-2 | *Long ago God spoke many times and in many ways to our ancestors through the prophets. And now in these final days, he has spoken to us through his Son.*

God communicates with you through his Son, Jesus Christ. Talk with him often throughout your day.

JOHN 14:26 | *When the Father sends the Advocate as my representative—that is, the Holy Spirit—he will teach you everything and will remind you of everything I have told you.*

ROMANS 8:16 | *His Spirit joins with our spirit to affirm that we are God's children.*

God communicates with you through his Holy Spirit. Pay special attention to the way he speaks to your heart and spirit.

ROMANS 2:14-15 | *Even Gentiles, who do not have God's written law, show that they know his law when they instinctively obey it, even without having heard it. They demonstrate that God's law is written in their hearts, for their own conscience and thoughts either accuse them or tell them they are doing right.*

God communicates with you through your conscience, which is your God-given internal radar to help you know right from wrong. Always listen to your conscience. If you neglect it, it will become dull and eventually you will no longer hear it.

PSALM 19:1-2 | *The heavens proclaim the glory of God. The skies display his craftsmanship. Day after day they continue to speak; night after night they make him known.*

ROMANS 1:19-20 | *They know the truth about God because he has made it obvious to them. For ever since the world was created, people have seen the earth and sky. Through everything God made, they can clearly see his invisible qualities—his eternal power and divine nature. So they have no excuse for not knowing God.*

God communicates with you through his creation. All nature sings about a majestic God who created the starry heavens, the roar of thunder, and the glorious snowcapped mountains. But nature also whispers about God's mind-boggling attention to detail in the wings of a butterfly, the variety of plants, and the complexity of a strand of DNA.

1 SAMUEL 3:7-10 | *Samuel did not yet know the LORD because he had never had a message from the LORD before. So the LORD called a third time, and once more Samuel got up and went to Eli. "Here I am. Did you call me?" Then Eli realized it was the LORD who was calling the boy. So he said to Samuel, "Go and lie down again, and if someone calls again, say, 'Speak, LORD, your servant is listening.'" So Samuel went back to bed. And the LORD came and called as before, "Samuel! Samuel!" And Samuel replied, "Speak, your servant is listening."*

God communicates with you through other people. Most of the time he uses godly people to give you spiritual advice and help you mature in your faith. But sometimes he uses people who don't know him to unwittingly communicate his truth to you.

How can I know when God is speaking to me?

JOHN 10:27 | *[Jesus said,] "My sheep listen to my voice; I know them, and they follow me."*

JOHN 14:21 | *[Jesus said,] "Those who accept my commandments and obey them are the ones who love me. And because they love me, my Father will love them. And I will love them and reveal myself to each of them."*

The best way to be certain of God's voice is to know God. If you don't know God, how could you recognize his voice?

JEREMIAH 15:16 | *When I discovered your words, I devoured them. They are my joy and my heart's delight.*

HEBREWS 4:12 | *The word of God is alive and powerful. It is sharper than the sharpest two-edged sword, cutting between soul and spirit, between joint and marrow. It exposes our innermost thoughts and desires.*

Just as a piano is tuned against a standard tuning fork, so you become in tune with God only when you compare yourself against the standards for living found in the Bible.

What does God want in my communication with him?

MARK 1:35 | *Before daybreak the next morning, Jesus got up and went out to an isolated place to pray.*

Prayer is finding the time to talk to God, as Jesus did, and building a relationship with him. But good conversation also includes listening—allowing God to speak to you. When you pray, take time to listen to him talk to you.

EPHESIANS 3:12 | *Because of Christ and our faith in him, we can now come boldly and confidently into God's presence.*

HEBREWS 10:22 | *Let us go right into the presence of God with sincere hearts fully trusting him.*

God wants you to approach him with confidence.

COLOSSIANS 4:2 | *Devote yourselves to prayer with an alert mind and a thankful heart.*

God wants you to make your communication with him a priority. Devote yourself to regular, consistent prayer.

PSALM 63:1-2 | *O God, you are my God; I earnestly search for you. My soul thirsts for you. . . . I have seen you in your sanctuary and gazed upon your power and glory.*

The more you know God, the more you long for him.

PHILIPPIANS 4:6 | *Don't worry about anything; instead, pray about everything. Tell God what you need, and thank him for all he has done.*

God wants you to communicate with him in an attitude of gratitude. What are the last three wonderful things God did for you? Have you thanked him?

Promise from God JOHN 10:27 | *[Jesus said,] "My sheep listen to my voice; I know them."*

COMPASSION

What can I learn about God's compassion to help me be more compassionate?

PSALM 79:8 | *Do not hold us guilty for the sins of our ancestors! Let your compassion quickly meet our needs, for we are on the brink of despair.*

Because God is compassionate, he meets your needs.

MATTHEW 14:14 | *Jesus saw the huge crowd as he stepped from the boat, and he had compassion on them and healed their sick.*

EPHESIANS 4:32 | *Be kind to each other, tenderhearted, forgiving one another, just as God through Christ has forgiven you.*

Because God is compassionate, he works in you to help you forgive others and to want to help them.

ISAIAH 54:7 | *For a brief moment I abandoned you, but with great compassion I will take you back.*

Because God is compassionate, he wants to have an eternal relationship with you.

How can I show compassion to others?

2 CORINTHIANS 8:9 | *You know the generous grace of our Lord Jesus Christ. Though he was rich, yet for your sakes he became poor, so that by his poverty he could make you rich.*

In his love and compassion for you, Jesus gave up his most high position to come to earth and die for your sins. Your goal, as a believer in Jesus, is to develop that same depth of love and compassion for others so that you would be willing to even give up your life for their sake.

JOB 5:27 | *[Eliphaz said,] "We have studied life and found all this to be true. Listen to my counsel, and apply it to yourself."*

Be very careful giving advice to hurting people; first they need compassion. Job's friends were not compassionate to him when he lost everything; thus, their advice was not helpful.

Promise from God PSALM 145:9 | *The LORD is good to everyone. He showers compassion on all his creation.*

COMPLACENCY

What causes me to grow complacent?

HOSEA 13:5-6 | *[God said,] "I took care of you in the wilderness, in that dry and thirsty land. But when you had eaten and were satisfied, you became proud and forgot me."*

When you are comfortable and prosperous and your basic needs are met, it could be easy for you to become complacent about God. Why would you need God if life is going your way? A wise person remembers God in times of both need *and* prosperity. You may be able to coast along without him for the present, but without God, you have no future.

How can complacency lead me to sin?

JAMES 4:17 | *Remember, it is sin to know what you ought to do and then not do it.*

To know what is right and then be complacent or unwilling to do it is sin. It's not enough to avoid doing wrong. God wants you to be proactive about doing what's right.

REVELATION 3:15-16 | *[God said,] "I know all the things you do, that you are neither hot nor cold. I wish that you were one or the other! But since you are like lukewarm water, neither hot nor cold, I will spit you out of my mouth!"*

Complacency leads to indifference, which leads to idleness. To stand for nothing is to not care. And to not care is to be apathetic and complacent about the needs of others. Complacency stands in stark contrast to God's command to love and care for those around you.

JUDGES 16:16-17 | *[Delilah] tormented him with her nagging day after day until he was sick to death of it. Finally, Samson shared his secret with her.*

Complacency makes you vulnerable to the strategies and temptations of Satan. Samson had become so complacent about his God-given responsibility as a leader that he gave in to Delilah's nagging and told her the secret to his strength.

1 KINGS 11:1-3 | *King Solomon loved many foreign women. . . . The LORD had clearly instructed the people of Israel, "You must not marry them, because they will turn your hearts to their gods." Yet Solomon insisted on loving them anyway. . . . And in fact, they did turn his heart away from the LORD.*

You will neglect God's Word if you are complacent toward it. Then you will not know what it says and how it can help you avoid danger. Solomon's complacency toward obeying God's commands led him into sin and its devastating consequences.

What must I never be complacent about?

DEUTERONOMY 6:5-6 | *You must love the LORD your God with all your heart, all your soul, and all your strength. And you must commit yourselves wholeheartedly to these commands that I am giving you today.*

LUKE 13:24 | *Work hard to enter the narrow door to God's Kingdom, for many will try to enter but will fail.*

Never be complacent about pursuing a relationship with God.

PHILIPPIANS 2:12-13 | *Work hard to show the results of your salvation, obeying God with deep reverence and fear. For God is working in you, giving you the desire and the power to do what pleases him.*

Never be complacent about obeying God's Word because obedience is the sign of a healthy relationship with him.

Promise from God DEUTERONOMY 4:29 | *If you search for [the Lord your God] with all your heart and soul, you will find him.*

COMPLAINING

Is it a sin to complain?

NUMBERS 21:5-6 | *[The people] began to speak against God and Moses. "Why have you brought us out of Egypt to die here in the wilderness?" they complained. "There is nothing to eat here and nothing to drink. And we hate this horrible manna!" So the LORD sent poisonous snakes among the people, and many were bitten and died.*

Complaining is a sin because it comes from selfishness. You are focusing on what you don't have, and in a real sense, coveting that. Complaining makes you a negative, nagging person.

What should I do instead of complaining?

PHILIPPIANS 2:14-15 | *Do everything without complaining and arguing, so that no one can criticize you. Live . . . as children of God, shining like bright lights in a world full of crooked and perverse people.*

Instead of complaining about others, say something positive about them. If you can't do that, then don't say anything at all. At least if you're quiet, you can't be blamed for being negative or critical.

LAMENTATIONS 3:39-40 | *Why should we, mere humans, complain when we are punished for our sins? Instead, let us test and examine our ways. Let us turn back to the LORD.*

Instead of complaining about the sins of others, focus on and repent of your own sins.

LUKE 6:37 | *Do not judge others, and you will not be judged. Do not condemn others, or it will all come back against you. Forgive others, and you will be forgiven.*

Instead of complaining about the mistakes of others, forgive them as you would like to be forgiven.

Promise from God EPHESIANS 4:29 | *Let everything you say be good and helpful, so that your words will be an encouragement to those who hear them.*

COMPROMISE

How do I live in today's culture without compromising my convictions?

DANIEL 1:8, 12-14 | *Daniel was determined not to defile himself by eating the food and wine given to them by the king. He asked the chief of staff for permission not to eat these unacceptable foods. . . . "Please test us for ten days on a diet of vegetables and water," Daniel said. "At the end of the ten days, see how*

*we look compared to the other young men who are eating the
king's food. Then make your decision in light of what you see."
The attendant agreed to Daniel's suggestion and tested them
for ten days.*

Never be afraid to take a stand for what you know is right
and true, but do so in a respectful, humble manner. You
will be surprised how often you will be admired for sticking
to your beliefs, even if others disagree with them. But even
if you meet resistance, you must not compromise by going
against God's Word.

EXODUS 34:12 | *Be very careful never to make a treaty with the
people who live in the land where you are going. If you do, you
will follow their evil ways and be trapped.*

HEBREWS 3:12-13 | *Be careful then, dear brothers and sisters.
Make sure that your own hearts are not evil and unbelieving,
turning you away from the living God. You must warn each
other every day, while it is still "today," so that none of you
will be deceived by sin and hardened against God.*

You must always be on the alert when living or working
with those who don't see sin as something wrong. You can
easily find yourself compromising and agreeing to commit
"little" sins. This will eventually dull your sensitivity to
other sins. A "little" sin now and then can lead to a life
defined by sin.

JUDGES 16:15-17 | *Delilah pouted, "How can you tell me, 'I love
you,' when you don't share your secrets with me? . . . You still
haven't told me what makes you so strong!" She tormented him*

with her nagging day after day until he was sick to death of it. Finally, Samson shared his secret with her.

You are most likely to compromise in areas where you are spiritually weak. Learn to recognize where you are vulnerable so that you are prepared when the temptation to compromise comes.

When is compromise appropriate, and how do I effectively compromise?

EZRA 10:3-4 | *We will follow the advice given by you and by the others who respect the commands of our God. Let it be done according to the Law of God. . . . It is your duty to tell us how to proceed in setting things straight. We are behind you, so be strong and take action.*

Within the will of God and the commands he has given in Scripture, it is healthy to give up something for the common good. But you must never give in if it means acting against God's Word. It is never appropriate to compromise the will of God as revealed in Scripture.

ROMANS 14:15 | *If another believer is distressed by what you eat, you are not acting in love if you eat it. Don't let your eating ruin someone for whom Christ died.*

ROMANS 15:1 | *We who are strong must be considerate of those who are sensitive about things like this. We must not just please ourselves.*

In order to maintain unity in the body of Christ, you as a Christian must be willing to avoid certain things. This may require compromising personal preferences, but never essential Christian beliefs.

Promise from God MATTHEW 10:32-33 | *[Jesus said,] "Everyone who acknowledges me publicly here on earth, I will also acknowledge before my Father in heaven. But everyone who denies me here on earth, I will also deny before my Father in heaven."*

CONFESSION

Does God truly forgive my sin when I confess it to him?

PSALM 32:5 | *Finally, I confessed all my sins to you and stopped trying to hide my guilt. I said to myself, "I will confess my rebellion to the LORD." And you forgave me! All my guilt is gone.*

1 JOHN 1:9 | *If we confess our sins to him, he is faithful and just to forgive us.*

Confession is the act of recognizing and admitting sin to God so he can forgive you. Confession indicates your desire to have your sins forgiven. If you have no desire to have your sins forgiven, God will not force his forgiveness on you. However, when you sincerely confess your sins to God, he fully forgives you.

PROVERBS 28:13 | *People who conceal their sins will not prosper, but if they confess and turn from them, they will receive mercy.*

Confession paves the way for God to work in you. Confession wipes the slate clean so that you can be reconciled to God and have another chance to live for him.

To whom do I confess my sins, God or others?

1 CHRONICLES 21:8 | *David said to God, "I have sinned greatly. . . . Please forgive my guilt for doing this foolish thing."*

We confess sin to God first, for only God can forgive sin.

JAMES 5:16 | *Confess your sins to each other and pray for each other so that you may be healed.*

It can be healing to confess sin to one another, especially if the others are committed to praying for you, encouraging you, and supporting you as you seek restoration. It is also important to confess sin to those whom you have wronged.

Promise from God 1 JOHN 1:9 | *If we confess our sins to him, he is faithful and just to forgive us our sins and to cleanse us from all wickedness.*

CONFLICT

What causes conflict?

2 SAMUEL 15:6, 12 | *Absalom . . . stole the hearts of all the people . . . and the conspiracy gained momentum.*

JAMES 4:2 | *You want what you don't have, so you scheme and kill to get it. You are jealous of what others have, but you can't get it, so you fight and wage war to take it away from them.*

Conflict begins when a person, group, or nation isn't getting what it wants and confronts whoever or whatever the obstacle is to try to get it. On a personal level, you want someone's behavior to be different, you want your way on some issue, you want to win, you want some possession, you want someone's loyalty. The list can go on and on. When another person isn't willing to give you what you want, you find yourself in conflict. Unresolved conflict can sometimes lead to open warfare. Conflict begins when people with opposing viewpoints are not willing to find common ground.

ESTHER 3:2, 5-6 | *Mordecai refused to bow. . . . [Haman] was filled with rage . . . so he decided it was not enough to lay hands on Mordecai alone. . . . He looked for a way to destroy all the Jews throughout the entire empire.*

Conflict begins when your pride is hurt and you begin to plot your revenge.

ROMANS 7:22-23 | *I love God's law with all my heart. But there is another power within me that is at war with my mind. This power makes me a slave to the sin that is still within me.*

Conflict begins when good confronts evil. The two cannot peacefully coexist, so a battle begins. Those who follow Christ experience conflict within themselves between the old sinful nature and the new spiritual nature.

MATTHEW 23:23-24 | *[Jesus said,] "What sorrow awaits you teachers of religious law and you Pharisees. Hypocrites! For you are careful to tithe even the tiniest income from your herb gardens, but you ignore the more important aspects of the law—justice, mercy, and faith. You should tithe, yes, but do not neglect the more important things. Blind guides! You strain your water so you won't accidentally swallow a gnat, but you swallow a camel!"*

There are times when you must not ignore certain situations and must actually initiate conflict in order to speak for truth and justice. This is healthy conflict. Jesus confronted the Pharisees not only for their hypocritical behavior but also because of their destructive influence as teachers and leaders.

What are some ways to resolve conflict?

GENESIS 13:7-9 | *Disputes broke out between the herdsmen of Abram and Lot. . . . Finally Abram said to Lot, "Let's not allow this conflict to come between us or our herdsmen. . . . Take your choice of any section of the land you want."*

Solving conflict takes initiative; someone must make the first move. Abram gave Lot first choice, putting family peace above personal desires.

GENESIS 26:21-22 | *Isaac's men then dug another well, but again there was a dispute over it. . . . Abandoning that one, Isaac moved on and dug another well. This time there was no dispute over it. . . . [Isaac] said, "At last the LORD has created enough space for us to prosper in this land."*

Solving conflict takes humility, persistence, and a preference for peace over personal victory.

2 SAMUEL 3:1 | *That was the beginning of a long war between those who were loyal to Saul and those loyal to David. As time passed David became stronger and stronger, while Saul's dynasty became weaker and weaker.*

Solving conflict involves compromise, finding common ground that is bigger than your differences. If neither side is willing to take the initiative or show the necessary humility to seek common ground, conflict will result in a broken friendship, divorce, or even war.

JOHN 17:21 | *I pray that they will all be one, just as you and I are one—as you are in me, Father, and I am in you. And may they be in us so that the world will believe you sent me.*

Praying for peace and unity with others makes a difference because you are seeking the help of the great Peacemaker.

How do I keep a conflict from getting out of control?

PROVERBS 17:27 | *A truly wise person uses few words; a person with understanding is even-tempered.*

Words can be used as tools or weapons and therefore must be used carefully.

MATTHEW 5:23-24 | *If you are presenting a sacrifice at the altar in the Temple and you suddenly remember that someone has something against you, leave your sacrifice there at the altar. Go and be reconciled to that person.*

We are not to "bury" or deny conflicts, but rather to take immediate steps to resolve them.

MATTHEW 18:15-17 | *[Jesus said,] "If another believer sins against you, go privately and point out the offense. If the other person listens and confesses it, you have won that person back. But if you are unsuccessful, take one or two others with you and go back again, so that everything you say may be confirmed by two or three witnesses. If the person still refuses to listen, take your case to the church."*

Jesus outlines a three-step process for confronting major conflicts among believers.

Promise from God   MATTHEW 5:9 | *God blesses those who work for peace, for they will be called the children of God.*

CONSCIENCE

Where does my conscience come from?

ROMANS 1:19-20 | *[People] know the truth about God because he has made it obvious to them. For ever since the world was created, people have seen the earth and sky. Through everything God made, they can clearly see his invisible qualities—his eternal power and divine nature. So they have no excuse for not knowing God.*

Conscience is the God-given instinct deep inside you that guides you to know right from wrong. It is the part of you that helps you understand if you are in line with God's will and God's Word.

How does my conscience really work? What does it do?

GENESIS 42:21 | *[Joseph's brothers] said, "Clearly we are being punished because of what we did to Joseph long ago. We saw his anguish when he pleaded for his life, but we wouldn't listen."*

Your conscience testifies against you to yourself, pointing out your sin and bringing a sense of guilt. It then urges you to remove this sense of guilt by righting the wrong. It is essential to listen to and obey your conscience or it will become dulled and useless.

Can I lose my conscience?

JUDGES 17:6 | *In those days Israel had no king; all the people did whatever seemed right in their own eyes.*

PROVERBS 29:7 | *The godly care about the rights of the poor; the wicked don't care at all.*

JEREMIAH 7:24 | *[The Lord said,] "But my people would not listen to me. They kept doing whatever they wanted, following the stubborn desires of their evil hearts. They went backward instead of forward."*

MICAH 3:1-2 | *Listen, you leaders of Israel! You are supposed to know right from wrong, but you are the very ones who hate good and love evil.*

You can't lose your conscience, but you can become so dulled to its urgings that you don't or can't hear it. The conscience is like a muscle; it must be exercised and developed. Without listening to your conscience, you feel free to do whatever you want. If you have a reputation for not always doing the right thing or if you find yourself unmoved by evil or injustice, it may be an indication that your conscience is becoming dulled or inactive. Those who have done horrible deeds still have a conscience, but over time they have learned to tune it out, allowing them to commit those heinous deeds.

How can I develop my conscience?

HOSEA 12:6 | *Come back to your God. Act with love and justice, and always depend on him.*

Even those who have rejected God can come back to him. When you commit yourself to God and live by the commands in his Word, he will restore your conscience.

Promise from God PSALM 119:105 | *Your word is a lamp to guide my feet and a light for my path.*

CONSEQUENCES

What are the consequences of choosing to sin?

ROMANS 6:23 | *The wages of sin is death.*

The greatest consequence of sin is death, or eternal separation from God.

GENESIS 3:16-17, 19 | *[The woman] took some of the fruit and ate it. Then she gave some to her husband, who was with her, and he ate it, too. . . . Then [God] said to the woman, "I will sharpen the pain of your pregnancy, and in pain you will give birth." . . . And to the man [God] said, ". . . The ground is cursed because of you. All your life you will struggle to scratch a living from it. . . . By the sweat of your brow will you have food to eat."*

Even a seemingly small sin must be looked at for what it is: disobedience to God. One of the realities of sin is that its effects spread, and like a ripple in a pond, the consequences get far beyond your control.

GALATIANS 6:7 | *You will always harvest what you plant.*

Sin is wrong, so it always produces bad consequences. God does not prevent you from acting foolishly, but he allows you to experience the consequences of your foolishness.

Do other people ever suffer the consequences of my sin?

JOSHUA 7:25 | *Joshua said to Achan, "Why have you brought trouble on us?"*

Your sinful actions affect more people than just yourself. Beware of the temptation to rationalize your sins by saying they are too small or too personal to hurt anyone but you.

EZEKIEL 3:16-17, 20 | *The LORD gave me a message. He said, "Son of man, I have appointed you as a watchman for Israel. Whenever you receive a message from me, warn people immediately. . . . If righteous people turn away from their righteous behavior and ignore the obstacles I put in their way, they will die. And if you do not warn them, they will die in their sins. None of their righteous acts will be remembered, and I will hold you responsible for their deaths."*

A watchman is guilty if he knows the enemy is coming and remains silent. You are guilty if you remain silent when you should warn others of the consequences of their actions.

ISAIAH 10:1-2 | *What sorrow awaits the unjust judges and those who issue unfair laws. They deprive the poor of justice and deny the rights of the needy among my people. They prey on widows and take advantage of orphans.*

The poor, widows, and orphans are often further hurt by others' sins of greed and injustice.

Can forgiveness of sin stop sin's consequences?

2 SAMUEL 12:13-14 | *David confessed to Nathan, "I have sinned against the LORD." Nathan replied, "Yes, but the LORD has*

forgiven you, and you won't die for this sin. Nevertheless . . . your child will die."

The consequences of sin are often irreversible. When God forgives you, he doesn't necessarily eliminate the consequences of your wrongdoing. He allows the natural consequences of your actions to happen. These consequences should be a powerful reminder for you when you face temptation again.

Can there also be positive consequences to my actions?

JOHN 3:16 | *God loved the world so much that he gave his one and only Son, so that everyone who believes in him will not perish but have eternal life.*

When you accept Jesus Christ as Savior and live faithfully for him, you will experience the positive consequences of eternal life as well as heavenly rewards.

JEREMIAH 17:7 | *Blessed are those who trust in the LORD and have made the LORD their hope and confidence.*

A life focused on God brings joy to God and many blessings to you. The more you trust and obey God, the more you will experience the blessings he gives.

HEBREWS 11:6 | *It is impossible to please God without faith. Anyone who wants to come to him must believe that God exists and that he rewards those who sincerely seek him.*

Looking for God brings the reward of experiencing his presence.

Promise from God ROMANS 6:23 | *The wages of sin is death, but the free gift of God is eternal life through Christ Jesus our Lord.*

CONTENTMENT

How can I find contentment, regardless of life's circumstances?

1 TIMOTHY 6:6-7 | *True godliness with contentment is itself great wealth. After all, we brought nothing with us when we came into the world, and we can't take anything with us when we leave it.*

Contentment comes from a proper perspective of eternity. Contentment is not how much you accumulate on earth but how much you send ahead to heaven. Who you are goes with you to eternity; what you have stays here.

PSALM 107:8-9 | *Let them praise the LORD for his great love and for the wonderful things he has done for them. For he satisfies the thirsty and fills the hungry with good things.*

ROMANS 8:38 | *I am convinced that nothing can ever separate us from God's love. Neither death nor life, neither angels nor demons, neither our fears for today nor our worries about tomorrow—not even the powers of hell can separate us from God's love.*

Contentment comes from the assurance that God loves you unconditionally. Nothing you do can make him love you more, and nothing you do can make him love you less.

PHILIPPIANS 4:11-13 | *Not that I was ever in need, for I have learned how to be content with whatever I have. I know how to live on almost nothing or with everything. I have learned the secret of living in every situation, whether it is with a full stomach or empty, with plenty or little. For I can do everything through Christ, who gives me strength.*

When contentment depends on things going your way, you become unhappy when things don't. When contentment comes from watching Jesus meet your needs, you are secure and happy because he never fails you. He teaches you to differentiate the valuable things in life from the distractions.

MATTHEW 5:3 | *God blesses those who are poor and realize their need for him, for the Kingdom of Heaven is theirs.*

LUKE 14:33 | *You cannot become my disciple without giving up everything you own.*

Contentment comes when you are willing to give up everything for God. Only then are you truly free to rest in the peace and security God offers. Contentment is not how much you have, but what you do for God with what you have.

GENESIS 27:41; 33:4, 9 | *Esau hated Jacob . . . and . . . began to scheme: "I will . . . kill my brother, Jacob." . . . [Later] Esau ran to meet [Jacob] and embraced him, threw his arms around his neck, and kissed him. And they both wept. . . . "My brother, I have plenty," Esau answered. "Keep what you have for yourself."*

Forgiving others is a key to contentment because it spares you the unhappiness that comes from holding a grudge.

What is the risk in being content?

HOSEA 13:6 | *When you had eaten and were satisfied, you became proud and forgot [the Lord your God].*

When contentment leads to complacency, you are in trouble. Enjoying God's blessings should lead you to stay close to him, not forget him; to thank him, not ignore him. You are at high risk when you find your ultimate contentment in things that fail the test of eternity—possessions, wealth, food, career, social position—because when they fail, your contentment ends.

Promise from God PSALM 107:9 | *[The Lord] satisfies the thirsty and fills the hungry with good things.*

CONVICTIONS

What are some basic convictions I must have to live out my faith effectively?

EXODUS 20:2-3 | *I am the LORD your God, who rescued you from the land of Egypt, the place of your slavery. You must not have any other god but me.*

Accept that God must have first priority in your life.

2 TIMOTHY 3:16 | *All Scripture is inspired by God and is useful to teach us what is true and to make us realize what is wrong in our lives. It corrects us when we are wrong and teaches us to do what is right.*

Believe that the Bible was written by God and is God's truth for all matters of faith and life.

ROMANS 4:21 | *He was fully convinced that God is able to do whatever he promises.*

Be assured that God always keeps his promises.

ROMANS 10:9 | *If you confess with your mouth that Jesus is Lord and believe in your heart that God raised him from the dead, you will be saved.*

2 CORINTHIANS 5:17 | *Anyone who belongs to Christ has become a new person. The old life is gone; a new life has begun!*

1 JOHN 1:9 | *If we confess our sins to him, he is faithful and just to forgive us our sins and to cleanse us from all wickedness.*

Accept that salvation is of God. If you are truly sorry for your sins and confess them to God (repentance) and if you believe that God's Son, Jesus, died for you, taking upon himself the punishment for sin you deserve, then God forgives you and gives you the gift of salvation. The moment this happens, the Holy Spirit enters your life and begins transforming you into a new person on the inside. Then you know that your life can and will be different.

EPHESIANS 4:15 | *We will speak the truth in love, growing in every way more and more like Christ.*

Be confident that if you live by the truths in God's Word, you will become more and more like Jesus, which is your primary goal.

ROMANS 8:39 | *No power in the sky above or in the earth below—indeed, nothing in all creation will ever be able to separate us from the love of God that is revealed in Christ Jesus our Lord.*

Know that nothing can separate you from God's love for you.

1 PETER 1:21 | *Through Christ you have come to trust in God. And you have placed your faith and hope in God because he raised Christ from the dead and gave him great glory.*

Remember that Christ has power over death, for he brought himself back from the dead.

PSALM 17:6 | *I am praying to you because I know you will answer, O God. Bend down and listen as I pray.*

Believe that God answers prayer.

PSALM 135:5 | *I know the greatness of the LORD—that our Lord is greater than any other god.*

Rest in the knowledge that no one is greater than God. He is sovereign and all-powerful.

Why is it important to have godly convictions?

DANIEL 1:8 | *Daniel was determined not to defile himself by eating the food and wine given to [him] by the king. He asked the chief of staff for permission not to eat these unacceptable foods.*

Convictions help you do what you believe is right.

EZRA 4:3 | *Zerubbabel, Jeshua, and the other leaders of Israel replied [to the enemies of Judah], "You may have no part in this work. We alone will build the Temple for the LORD, the God of Israel."*

Convictions help you avoid compromising with those who want to influence your values negatively.

EXODUS 20:6 | *[God said,] "I lavish unfailing love for a thousand generations on those who love me and obey my commands."*

Convictions help you experience more of God's blessing.

1 JOHN 3:21 | *If we don't feel guilty, we can come to God with bold confidence.*

Convictions help you approach God confidently.

EPHESIANS 4:13-15 | *[Equipping and building up the church] will continue until we all come to such unity in our faith and knowledge of God's Son that we will be mature in the Lord, measuring up to the full and complete standard of Christ. Then we will no longer be immature like children. We won't be tossed and blown about by every wind of new teaching. We will not be influenced when people try to trick us with lies so clever they sound like the truth. Instead, we will speak the truth in love, growing in every way more and more like Christ.*

Convictions help you become more like Christ.

How do I live out my convictions?

PSALM 119:7 | *As I learn your righteous regulations, I will thank you by living as I should!*

PSALM 143:8 | *Let me hear of your unfailing love each morning, for I am trusting you. Show me where to walk, for I give myself to you.*

You live out your convictions by making daily decisions to obey God's Word, the standard for your convictions.

DANIEL 3:16-18 | *Shadrach, Meshach, and Abednego replied, "O Nebuchadnezzar, we do not need to defend ourselves before you. If we are thrown into the blazing furnace, the God whom we serve is able to save us. . . . But even if he doesn't, we want to make it clear to you, Your Majesty, that we will never serve your gods or worship the gold statue you have set up."*

You live out your convictions by not compromising your conscience and by keeping God your main focus.

DANIEL 1:8 | *Daniel was determined not to defile himself by eating the food and wine given to [him] by the king. He asked the chief of staff for permission not to eat these unacceptable foods.*

You live out your convictions by respectfully negotiating issues with others without compromising your values.

2 CORINTHIANS 4:13 | *We continue to preach because we have the same kind of faith the psalmist had when he said, "I believed in God, so I spoke."*

You live out your convictions with faith that God is real and his message in the Bible is true.

1 CORINTHIANS 9:19-23 | *Even though I am a free man with no master, I have become a slave to all people to bring many to Christ. When I was with the Jews, I lived like a Jew to bring the Jews to Christ. . . . When I am with the Gentiles who do not follow the Jewish law, I too live apart from that law so I can bring them to Christ. But I do not ignore the law of God; I obey the law of Christ. When I am with those who are weak, I share their weakness, for I want to bring the weak to Christ. Yes, I try to find common ground with everyone, doing*

everything I can to save some. I do everything to spread the
Good News and share in its blessings.

You live out your conviction that your goal is to bring others
to Christ.

Promise from God ROMANS 2:7 | *He will give eternal life to*
those who keep on doing good, seeking after the glory and honor
and immortality that God offers.

COURAGE

Where do I get the courage to go on when life seems too hard or obstacles seem too big?

ISAIAH 41:10 | *Don't be afraid, for I am with you. Don't be*
discouraged, for I am your God. I will strengthen you and help
you. I will hold you up with my victorious right hand.

Throughout your life you will find yourself in scary situations—mortal danger, extreme stress, major illness, money
issues, or any number of problems. True courage comes
from understanding that God is stronger than your biggest
problem or strongest enemy, and knowing that he wants
you to use his power to help you. Courage is not misplaced
confidence in your own strength, but well-placed confidence in God's strength.

Will God take away the things that frighten me?

NUMBERS 14:6-7, 9 | *Two of the men who had explored the land,*
Joshua son of Nun and Caleb son of Jephunneh, . . . said to all

the people . . . "The land we traveled through and explored is a wonderful land! . . . Don't be afraid of the people of the land. . . . They have no protection, but the LORD is with us! Don't be afraid of them!"

Fear is part of life and comes from feeling alone against a great threat. God may not take away things that frighten you, but he will give you courage by being beside you helping you fight the threat. Joshua and Caleb had courage, fueled by the promise that God was greater than any enemy or problem they faced.

ACTS 4:24, 29-31 | *When they heard the report, all the believers lifted their voices together in prayer to God: ". . . O Lord, hear their threats, and give us, your servants, great boldness in preaching your word. Stretch out your hand with healing power; may miraculous signs and wonders be done through the name of your holy servant Jesus." After this prayer, the meeting place shook, and they were all filled with the Holy Spirit. Then they preached the word of God with boldness.*

The early church was constantly threatened by religious persecution. The believers did not pray for the threats to end, but for the courage to face them. Sometimes God will remove the things that frighten you. But often, the Holy Spirit will give you the boldness to turn those threats into opportunities for spiritual growth and for declaring your faith.

JOB 11:18 | *Having hope will give you courage.*

Hope helps you see beyond the immediate crisis. If God took away everything that frightened you, there would be no need for hope in your life. And it is through hope you accept Christ as Savior and place your eternal future in his hands.

Are there consequences to a lack of courage?

LUKE 23:21-24 | *[The mob] kept shouting, "Crucify him! Crucify him!" For the third time [Pilate] demanded, "Why? What crime has he committed? I have found no reason to sentence him to death. So I will have him flogged, and then I will release him." But the mob shouted louder and louder, demanding that Jesus be crucified, and their voices prevailed. So Pilate sentenced Jesus to die as they demanded.*

Standing up for what is right can get you in trouble with corrupt people. Failing to stand up for what is right can get you in trouble with God. Pilate gave in to the demands of corrupt people and sentenced God's Son to death.

Promise from God JOSHUA 1:9 | *Be strong and courageous! Do not be afraid or discouraged. For the LORD your God is with you wherever you go.*

CRITICISM

How should I respond to criticism? How do I evaluate whether it is constructive or destructive?

PROVERBS 12:16-18 | *A wise person stays calm when insulted. An honest witness tells the truth; a false witness tells lies. Some people make cutting remarks, but the words of the wise bring healing.*

Stay calm and don't lash back. Measure criticism according to the character of the person who is giving it. Ask yourself if the criticism is meant to heal or hurt.

1 CORINTHIANS 4:4 | *My conscience is clear, but that doesn't prove I'm right. It is the Lord himself who will examine me and decide.*

Always work to maintain a clear conscience by being honest and trustworthy. This allows you to shrug off criticism you know is unjustified.

1 PETER 4:14 | *Be happy when you are insulted for being a Christian, for then the glorious Spirit of God rests upon you.*

Consider it a privilege to be criticized for your faith in God. God has special blessings for those who patiently endure this kind of criticism.

PROVERBS 15:31-32 | *If you listen to constructive criticism, you will be at home among the wise. If you reject discipline, you only harm yourself; but if you listen to correction, you grow in understanding.*

Don't reject truthful information that will help you grow. This requires a great deal of humility because accepting criticism is a hard thing to do. Sometimes it's painful to hear the truth, but it's worse to continue harmful behavior.

PROVERBS 15:1 | *A gentle answer deflects anger, but harsh words make tempers flare.*

When unjustly criticized, respond gently with the truth. Getting angry and defensive will only make the criticism seem true.

How do I offer criticism appropriately?

JOHN 8:7 | *Let the one who has never sinned throw the first stone!*

ROMANS 2:1 | *When you say they are wicked and should be punished, you are condemning yourself, for you who judge others do these very same things.*

Before criticizing another, take an inventory of your own sins and shortcomings so that you can approach the person with understanding and humility.

1 CORINTHIANS 13:5 | *[Love] does not demand its own way. It is not irritable, and it keeps no record of being wronged.*

Constructive criticism is always offered in love, with the motivation to build up. It addresses a specific need in someone else, not a list of his or her shortcomings or character flaws.

Promise from God ROMANS 14:17-18 | *The Kingdom of God is . . . living a life of goodness and peace and joy in the Holy Spirit. If you serve Christ with this attitude [of goodness and peace and joy in the Holy Spirit], you will please God, and others will approve of you, too.*

DEATH

What will happen to me when I die?

1 CORINTHIANS 15:53 | *Our dying bodies must be transformed into bodies that will never die; our mortal bodies must be transformed into immortal bodies.*

1 THESSALONIANS 4:13, 16-17 | *Dear brothers and sisters, we want you to know what will happen to the believers who have died so you will not grieve like people who have no hope. . . . For the Lord himself will come down from heaven with a commanding shout. . . . First, the Christians who have died will rise from their graves. Then, together with them, we who are still alive and remain on the earth will be caught up in the clouds to meet the Lord in the air. Then we will be with the Lord forever.*

REVELATION 21:3 | *Look, God's home is now among his people! He will live with them, and they will be his people. God himself will be with them.*

A Christian who dies will meet God face to face and live with him forever. Your body will be totally transformed into one that will never again be subjected to sin, pain, and the limitations of this world.

JOHN 11:25-26 | *[Jesus said,] "I am the resurrection and the life. Anyone who believes in me will live, even after dying. Everyone who lives in me and believes in me will never ever die."*

ROMANS 8:10 | *Christ lives within you, so even though your body will die because of sin, the Spirit gives you life because you have been made right with God.*

For those who believe that Jesus is their Savior, death is not the end but only the beginning of an eternity of unspeakable joy with the Lord and with other believers.

How do I keep a proper perspective about death? Why am I so afraid of it?

2 CORINTHIANS 5:4 | *While we live in these earthly bodies, we groan and sigh, but it's not that we want to die and get rid of these bodies that clothe us. Rather, we want to put on our new bodies so that these dying bodies will be swallowed up by life.*

COLOSSIANS 3:1-3 | *Since you have been raised to new life with Christ, set your sights on the realities of heaven. . . . Think about the things of heaven, not the things of earth. For you died to this life, and your real life is . . . with Christ in God.*

Fear of the unknown is natural, but obsession with it is not healthy. Fear of death can be useful when it draws you closer to God and causes you to make every day count for him. It is helpful to think of death as a beginning, not an end. It is your entrance into eternal life with God.

PHILIPPIANS 1:21 | *Living means living for Christ, and dying is even better.*

Fear of dying may be an indication of a weak relationship with God, a misunderstanding of heaven, or a lack of perspective that what you do here on earth affects how you live eternally. The more real God is to you, the less fearsome death will be.

ROMANS 8:10 | *Christ lives within you, so even though your body will die because of sin, the Spirit gives you life because you have been made right with God.*

When you accept Jesus Christ as Lord of your life, you are given the gift of eternal life. This does not prevent the death of your earthly body, but it does guarantee that God will give you a new body in which your spirit will continue to live forever in heaven and where there is no aging and no more death or sickness (see Revelation 21:4).

Promise from God JOHN 11:25 | *Jesus [said], "I am the resurrection and the life. Anyone who believes in me will live, even after dying."*

DECEIT/DECEPTION

How can I know when I'm being deceived?

JUDGES 16:6 | *Delilah said to Samson, "Please tell me what makes you so strong and what it would take to tie you up securely."*

Ask yourself if your conscience still has a strong voice inside you. When your conscience tells you no and your desire tells you yes, can you still hear and follow your conscience? In this case, Delilah's beauty and promise of sexual pleasure convinced Samson that she was sincere. Samson was the spiritual leader of Israel, yet he was spending the evening in the home of an ungodly woman who was sexually tempting him. What had happened to his conscience? When you make a practice of not listening to your conscience, soon you will hardly hear it.

ACTS 17:11 | *They searched the Scriptures day after day to see if Paul and Silas were teaching the truth.*

2 TIMOTHY 3:16 | *All Scripture is inspired by God and is useful to teach us what is true and to make us realize what is wrong in our lives. It corrects us when we are wrong and teaches us to do what is right.*

If someone is trying to convince you to do something that contradicts Scripture, you can be assured it is wrong. Know the Bible well enough to discern when someone is telling you something false.

GENESIS 3:6 | *The woman was convinced. She saw that the tree was beautiful and its fruit looked delicious, and she wanted the wisdom it would give her. So she took some of the fruit and ate it.*

If something seems too good to be true, ask yourself if you are being deceived. Sometimes you are wildly blessed and it is for real. But most often, if something sounds too good to be true, it isn't true.

PROVERBS 14:7 | *Stay away from fools, for you won't find knowledge on their lips.*

How often we ignore obvious truths! Stay away from deceitful people if you want to keep from being deceived.

2 TIMOTHY 3:13 | *Evil people and impostors will flourish. They will deceive others and will themselves be deceived.*

As long as Satan has power to deceive, he will deceive people, and they in turn will try to deceive you. The worst kind of deceiver is the false teacher, who appears to give good advice but actually will lead you down a path to destruction.

How do I deceive myself?

JEREMIAH 17:9 | *The human heart is the most deceitful of all things.*

GALATIANS 6:7 | *Don't be misled—you cannot mock the justice of God. You will always harvest what you plant.*

You deceive yourself when you think you can get away with sin, and you deceive yourself when you think you can ignore God and still receive his blessings.

1 CORINTHIANS 3:18 | *Stop deceiving yourselves. If you think you are wise by this world's standards, you need to become a fool to be truly wise.*

You deceive yourself when you live as though this world is all there is. And you deceive yourself when you buy into the morals and values of your culture without evaluating them through the filter of God's Word.

Promise from God PSALM 32:2 | *What joy for those whose record the LORD has cleared of guilt, whose lives are lived in complete honesty!*

DECISIONS

What are some principles of good decision making?

ROMANS 2:18 | *You know what [God] wants; you know what is right because you have been taught his law.*

Start by making the basic and obvious decisions to do what the Bible says is right and to avoid what the Bible says is wrong. You can't make big, complicated decisions well if you haven't practiced the fundamental ones. For example, if you have decided to consistently tell the truth, then saying no to a tantalizing job opportunity will be a much easier decision if you know the company's environment will encourage you to tell little lies to get ahead.

PROVERBS 18:13 | *Spouting off before listening to the facts is both shameful and foolish.*

Make sure you have all the facts.

PROVERBS 18:15 | *Intelligent people are always ready to learn. Their ears are open for knowledge.*

Be open to ideas.

LUKE 6:12-13 | *Jesus went up on a mountain to pray, and he prayed to God all night. At daybreak he called together all of his disciples and chose twelve of them to be apostles.*

1 JOHN 5:14 | *We are confident that he hears us whenever we ask for anything that pleases him.*

Saturate your life with prayer as you seek God's guidance. Talking with God calms your spirit and clears your mind, making you more able to hear his counsel.

PROVERBS 12:15 | *Fools think their own way is right, but the wise listen to others.*

Seek the advice of trusted friends.

MATTHEW 16:26 | *What do you benefit if you gain the whole world but lose your own soul? Is anything worth more than your soul?*

Resist the temptation to make choices guided by a desire for personal satisfaction. Such ambition will lead you to make some very bad decisions.

Should I "put out a fleece"?

JUDGES 6:39 | *Gideon said to God, ". . . This time let the fleece remain dry while the ground around it is wet with dew."*

"Putting out a fleece" means that you designate a sign that will confirm you made the right decision and then ask God to make that sign occur. Great caution must be exercised when putting out a fleece because it tends to limit the options of a God who has unlimited options available to you. It is also dangerous because it can be used to blame God if the decision doesn't go the way you wanted. Let God decide, from his unlimited options, how best to lead you.

What is the most important decision I can make?

JOSHUA 24:15 | *Choose today whom you will serve. . . . As for me and my family, we will serve the LORD.*

JOHN 3:16 | *God loved the world so much that he gave his one and only Son, so that everyone who believes in him will not perish but have eternal life.*

The most important decision you, or anyone else, will make is whether or not you will be a follower of the one true God. This decision requires believing that his Son, Jesus, died for your sins and rose from the dead so that you can have a relationship with God forever. This is a decision that has eternal implications.

Promise from God   PROVERBS 3:6 | *Seek [the Lord's] will in all you do, and he will show you which path to take.*

DEPRESSION

Does God care when I feel depressed?

PSALM 34:18 | *The LORD is close to the brokenhearted; he rescues those whose spirits are crushed.*

MATTHEW 5:4 | *God blesses those who mourn, for they will be comforted.*

God isn't disappointed by your depression and emotional struggles; on the contrary, he feels a special closeness to you. You can actually experience more of God's presence in times of brokenness.

PSALM 139:12 | *Even in darkness I cannot hide from you.*

There is no depth to which you can descend where God is not present with you. Even if you don't feel his presence, he has not abandoned you. You don't have to feel trapped in the darkness if you allow God's comforting light to enter your soul.

PSALM 130:1 | *From the depths of despair, O LORD, I call for your help.*

Allow yourself to cry out to God even from the darkest pit of despair. He wants to help you.

ISAIAH 53:3 | *He was despised and rejected—a man of sorrows, acquainted with deepest grief.*

Remember that Jesus understands the pain of human life, and he suffered everything you have and more.

ROMANS 8:39 | *No power in the sky above or in the earth below— indeed, nothing in all creation will ever be able to separate us from the love of God that is revealed in Christ Jesus our Lord.*

Not even life's worst depression can separate you from the love Jesus has for you and wants to lavish on you. He knows all that has happened and what you are going through, and he loves you with a greater love than you could ever imagine.

Does feeling depressed mean something is wrong with my faith?

JUDGES 15:18 | *Samson was now very thirsty, and he cried out to the LORD, "You have accomplished this great victory by the strength of your servant. Must I now die of thirst . . . ?"*

1 KINGS 19:3-4 | *Elijah was afraid and fled for his life. . . . He sat down under a solitary broom tree and prayed that he might die.*

Even for the people of God, depression can often follow great achievement or spiritual victory. You are on such a high that the only place to go is down. This is common, and if you recognize this, you will not be surprised when you feel down soon after feeling on top of the world.

PSALM 40:2 | *[The Lord] lifted me out of the pit of despair. . . . He set my feet on solid ground and steadied me as I walked along.*

MATTHEW 14:30-31 | *When [Peter] saw the strong wind and the waves, he was terrified and began to sink. "Save me, Lord!" he shouted. Jesus immediately reached out and grabbed him.*

God is able to lift you out of the pit of depression and fear, but you must let him. There is something wrong with your faith only if you convince yourself that God cannot or does not want to help you.

Can any good come out of my depression?

PSALM 126:5 | *Those who plant in tears will harvest with shouts of joy.*

2 CORINTHIANS 12:9 | *[God] said, "My grace is all you need. My power works best in weakness." So now I am glad to boast about my weaknesses, so that the power of Christ can work through me.*

When you are weak, you are more receptive to the Lord's strength. When everything is going your way, it's easy to overlook God's hand in your life. As God works through your weakness, however, you learn to depend more on him and recognize and be grateful for the good work that only he can accomplish in you.

How can I help people who are depressed?

PROVERBS 25:20 | *Singing cheerful songs to a person with a heavy heart is like taking someone's coat in cold weather or pouring vinegar in a wound.*

ROMANS 12:15 | *Be happy with those who are happy, and weep with those who weep.*

2 CORINTHIANS 1:4 | *[God] comforts us in all our troubles so that we can comfort others.*

The best way to help people who are down is to model the gentle, caring love of Christ. Those dealing with depression need comfort and understanding, not advice and lectures. You can help those who are depressed by your quiet presence, your love, and your encouragement. Telling them to "snap out of it" or minimizing their pain by false cheeriness will just make them feel worse.

Promise from God MATTHEW 11:28-30 | *Jesus said, "Come to me, all of you who are weary and carry heavy burdens, and I will give you rest. Take my yoke upon you. Let me teach you, because I am humble and gentle at heart, and you will find rest for your souls. For my yoke is easy to bear, and the burden I give you is light."*

DESIRES

Is it okay to want something?

1 KINGS 3:5 | *The LORD appeared to Solomon in a dream, and God said, "What do you want? Ask, and I will give it to you!"*

PROVERBS 13:12 | *Hope deferred makes the heart sick, but a dream fulfilled is a tree of life.*

God created desire within you as a means of expressing yourself. Desire is good and healthy if directed toward the proper object: that which is good and right and God-honoring. It is ironic that a desire can be right or wrong, depending upon your motive and the object of your desire. For example, loving someone of the opposite sex, if directed to your spouse, is healthy and right. But that same desire directed to someone who is not your spouse is adultery. The desire to lead an organization is healthy if your motive is to serve others, but unhealthy and wrong if your motive is the power to control others.

PSALM 73:25 | *I desire [God] more than anything on earth.*

ISAIAH 26:8 | *LORD, we show our trust in you by obeying your laws; our heart's desire is to glorify your name.*

Your greatest desire must be a relationship with God because that will influence all your other desires.

PHILIPPIANS 4:8 | *Fix your thoughts on what is true, and honorable, and right, and pure, and lovely, and admirable. Think about things that are excellent and worthy of praise.*

Desiring sin is always wrong. Make sure the object of your desire is good, consistent with God's Word, and helpful to others.

How do I resist evil desires?

JAMES 3:13 | *If you are wise and understand God's ways, prove it by living an honorable life, doing good works with the humility that comes from wisdom.*

Keep yourself busy with good deeds.

MATTHEW 6:13 | *Don't let us yield to temptation, but rescue us from the evil one.*

Pray that good desires will overcome bad ones.

2 CHRONICLES 34:33 | *Josiah removed all detestable idols from the entire land.*

Take away the source of temptation.

COLOSSIANS 3:2 | *Think about the things of heaven, not the things of earth.*

Fill your mind with God and thoughts that honor him.

PROVERBS 15:22 | *Plans go wrong for lack of advice; many advisers bring success.*

Find a person willing to help you. You (and everyone else) need someone who will encourage you and hold you accountable.

Can God help me change the desires within my heart? How?

ROMANS 7:6 | *We can serve God, not in the old way . . . but in the new way of living in the Spirit.*

When you give control of your life to God, he gives you a new heart, a new nature, and a new desire to please him.

EZRA 1:5 | *God stirred the hearts of the priests and Levites . . . to go to Jerusalem to rebuild the Temple of the LORD.*

God stirs your heart with right desires. It is up to you to ask him for help to act upon them.

Promise from God EZEKIEL 36:26 | *[The sovereign Lord said,] "I will give you a new heart, and I will put a new spirit in you. I will take out your stony, stubborn heart and give you a tender, responsive heart."*

DOUBT

Is it a sin to doubt God? Does it mean I am lacking faith?

GENESIS 15:8 | *Abram [said], "O Sovereign LORD, how can I be sure?"*

PSALM 94:19 | *When doubts filled my mind, your comfort gave me renewed hope and cheer.*

MATTHEW 14:31 | *Jesus immediately reached out and grabbed [Peter]. "You have so little faith," Jesus said. "Why did you doubt me?"*

David, John the Baptist, and Peter, along with many other biblical heroes, struggled with various doubts about God and his ability or desire to help. God doesn't mind doubt as long as you are seeking answers from him in the midst of it. Doubt can become sin if it leads you away from God to skepticism, to cynicism, then to hard-heartedness. Allow your doubt to move you closer to God, not further away from him. As you move closer to him, you will find the strength to trust him and your faith will grow even stronger.

GENESIS 3:4 | *"You won't die!" the serpent replied to the woman.*

One of Satan's tactics is to get you to doubt God's goodness. He tries to get you to forget all God has given you and to focus on what you don't have. If you are spending much of your time thinking about what you don't have, you may be slipping into unhealthy doubt.

What should I do when I find myself doubting God?

HABAKKUK 1:2 | *How long, O LORD, must I call for help?*

Bring your doubts directly to God in prayer. Be candid and honest as you pour out your heart to the Lord.

MARK 9:24 | *The father instantly cried out, "I do believe, but help me overcome my unbelief!"*

Pray that God will give you the strong faith you need.

DEUTERONOMY 7:18 | *Don't be afraid . . . ! Just remember what the LORD your God did to Pharaoh and to all the land of Egypt.*

MARK 8:17-19 | *[Jesus] said, "Why are you [so worried] about having no bread? . . . Don't you remember anything at all? When I fed the 5,000 with five loaves of bread, how many baskets of leftovers did you pick up afterward?"*

When you are struggling with doubt, take time to remember the way God has worked in your life. As you recall God's "track record," you will grow confident that he will work in your present situation as well.

JOHN 20:27 | *[Jesus] said to Thomas, "Put your finger here, and look at my hands. Put your hand into the wound in my side. Don't be faithless any longer. Believe!"*

When you have doubts, review the evidence. There is a great deal of historical evidence to verify the accuracy of the Bible's claims.

HABAKKUK 2:1 | *I will wait to see what the LORD says and how he will answer my complaint.*

Be patient. Let God answer your questions on his schedule, not yours. Don't throw away your faith just because God doesn't resolve your doubt immediately.

1 THESSALONIANS 5:11 | *Encourage each other and build each other up, just as you are already doing.*

HEBREWS 10:25 | *Let us not neglect our meeting together.*

When you are wrestling with doubt, keep attending church and stay close to other Christians. Resist the temptation to isolate yourself, for that will only serve to weaken your faith more. Doubt feeds on loneliness.

Are there things I should never doubt?

JOHN 6:37 | *[Jesus said,] "Those the Father has given me will come to me, and I will never reject them."*

JOHN 10:28-29 | *[Jesus said,] "I give them eternal life, and they will never perish. No one can snatch them away from me, for my Father has given them to me, and he is more powerful than anyone else. No one can snatch them from the Father's hand."*

EPHESIANS 1:14 | *The Spirit is God's guarantee that he will give us the inheritance he promised and that he has purchased us to be his own people.*

Never doubt your salvation. Once you become a Christian, Satan can never snatch you away from God.

2 CORINTHIANS 6:2 | *God says, "At just the right time, I heard you. On the day of salvation, I helped you." Indeed, the "right time" is now. Today is the day of salvation.*

Never doubt God's desire or ability to help you.

Promise from God HEBREWS 13:5 | *God has said, "I will never fail you. I will never abandon you."*

ENCOURAGEMENT

How can I be an encouragement to others?

1 SAMUEL 23:16 | *Jonathan went to find David and encouraged him to stay strong in his faith in God.*

Through your words and example you can inspire others to stay close to God.

EZRA 5:1-2 | *Haggai and Zechariah . . . prophesied to the Jews in Judah and Jerusalem. . . . Zerubbabel . . . responded by starting again to rebuild the Temple of God in Jerusalem. And the prophets of God were with them and helped them.*

Sometimes encouragement means getting a person involved once again in productive work.

ACTS 11:23 | *[Barnabas] encouraged the believers to stay true to the Lord.*

Encourage others to hold fast to the principles of faith and to take action with those principles. Barnabas is known as the "Son of Encouragement" in the Bible (see Acts 4:36). Barnabas's encouragement of John Mark helped him become a great leader in the church (see Acts 15:36-39).

PHILEMON 1:11 | *He is very useful to both of us.*

Show others you trust them.

PHILIPPIANS 1:6 | *I am certain that God, who began the good work within you, will continue his work until it is finally finished.*

Remind others of what God wants to do in them and through them.

JOSHUA 24:2, 13 | *Joshua said to the people, "This is what the LORD, the God of Israel says: . . . I gave you land you had not worked on, and I gave you towns you did not build—the towns where you are now living. I gave you vineyards and olive groves for food, though you did not plant them."*

Review God's past blessings with others.

JOB 29:24 | *When they were discouraged, I smiled at them. My look of approval was precious to them.*

Sometimes just a smile is a great encouragement.

How does God encourage me?

MATTHEW 9:22 | *Jesus . . . said, "Daughter, be encouraged! Your faith has made you well." And the woman was healed at that moment.*

He heals your wounds and renews your faith.

PSALM 138:3 | *As soon as I pray, you answer me; you encourage me by giving me strength.*

God responds when you talk to him and gives you strength when you are weak.

PSALM 119:25, 28 | *I lie in the dust; revive me by your word. . . . I weep with sorrow; encourage me by your word.*

ROMANS 15:4 | *The Scriptures give us hope and encouragement as we wait patiently for God's promises to be fulfilled.*

He revives you and gives you hope as you read his written Word.

HEBREWS 12:5 | *Have you forgotten the encouraging words God spoke to you as his children? He said, "My child, don't make light of the LORD's discipline, and don't give up when he corrects you."*

Be encouraged that God loves you enough to correct you and keep you on the best path for your life.

Promise from God 2 THESSALONIANS 2:16-17 | *May our Lord Jesus Christ himself and God our Father, who loved us and by his grace gave us eternal comfort and a wonderful hope, comfort you and strengthen you in every good thing you do and say.*

ENEMIES

What does it mean to love my enemies?

MATTHEW 5:43-44 | *[Jesus said,] "You have heard the law that says, 'Love your neighbor' and hate your enemy. But I say, love your enemies! Pray for those who persecute you!"*

ROMANS 12:20-21 | *If your enemies are hungry, feed them. If they are thirsty, give them something to drink. In doing this, you will heap burning coals of shame on their heads. Don't let evil conquer you, but conquer evil by doing good.*

Loving your enemies is always unreasonable—unless you realize that you were an enemy of God until he forgave you. When you love an enemy, you see him or her as Christ does—a person in need of grace. Getting to that point takes prayer. You can't pray for people and not feel compassion for them.

MATTHEW 18:21-22 | *Peter . . . asked, "Lord, how often should I forgive someone who sins against me? Seven times?" "No, not seven times," Jesus replied, "but seventy times seven!"*

Respond to your enemies with forgiveness—no matter what they try to do.

Is it possible to turn an enemy into a friend?

ACTS 9:1-6 | *Saul was uttering threats with every breath and was eager to kill the Lord's followers. . . . He wanted to bring them— both men and women—back to Jerusalem in chains. As he was approaching Damascus on this mission, a light from heaven suddenly shone down around him. He fell to the ground and heard a voice saying to him, "Saul! Saul! Why are you persecuting me?" "Who are you, lord?" Saul asked. And the voice replied, "I am Jesus, the one you are persecuting! Now get up and go into the city, and you will be told what you must do."*

GALATIANS 1:23 | *People were saying, "The one who used to persecute us is now preaching the very faith he tried to destroy!"*

Every day enemies of God become believers in God! It is a mystery why he overwhelms some enemies, such as Saul (whose name was changed to Paul), so that they turn to his side and why he seems to leave other enemies alone, at least in this world. But in almost every church around the world there are believers who once actively opposed God, God's people, and God's way of living.

1 PETER 2:12 | *Be careful to live properly among your unbelieving neighbors. Then even if they accuse you of doing wrong, they will see your honorable behavior, and they will give honor to God when he judges the world.*

There is nothing more powerful and effective than an enemy who has become a friend. With love, forgiveness, prayer, and kind words, you will be able to turn some of your enemies into your friends.

Are there really spiritual enemies—powers of darkness—trying to attack me?

DANIEL 10:12-13 | *[The man in the vision] said, "Don't be afraid, Daniel. Since the first day you began to pray for understanding and to humble yourself before your God, your request has been heard in heaven. I have come in answer to your prayer. But for twenty-one days the spirit prince of the kingdom of Persia blocked my way. Then Michael, one of the archangels, came to help me."*

MATTHEW 4:1 | *Jesus was led by the Spirit into the wilderness to be tempted there by the devil.*

The Bible clearly teaches that human beings are involved in a spiritual battle. Far from excluding you from this spiritual battle, faith puts you right in the middle of it. You are in a battle for your very soul. You must recognize that and arm yourself or you will be defeated.

EPHESIANS 6:12 | *We are not fighting against flesh-and-blood enemies, but against evil rulers and authorities of the unseen world, against mighty powers in this dark world, and against evil spirits in the heavenly places.*

The intent of evil is to defy God and wear down believers until they are led into sin. This gives Satan pleasure and greater power. But God is a Warrior. A battle rages in the spiritual realm, and as a believer, you are right in the thick of it. God is always ready to fight on your behalf, always ready to come to your defense. In addition, he provides you with armor so that you can fight alongside him (see Ephesians 6:11-18). But you must join God in the battle or you will be vulnerable and helpless to withstand the enemy. If you join, you are guaranteed victory.

Promise from God 2 THESSALONIANS 3:3 | *The Lord is faithful; he will strengthen you and guard you from the evil one.*

ENVIRONMENT

What does the Bible say about the environment and my responsibility in environmental issues?

GENESIS 1:28 | *God blessed [the human beings] and said, "Be fruitful and multiply. Fill the earth and govern it. Reign over . . . all the animals."*

Human beings were created to share responsibility for the earth by being good stewards of the created environment.

GENESIS 2:15 | *The LORD God placed the man in the Garden of Eden to tend and watch over it.*

The first assignment God gave to Adam was to tend and care for the Garden of Eden, and God expects you to care for your little corner of the earth as well.

DEUTERONOMY 20:19 | *When you are attacking a town and the war drags on, you must not cut down the trees. . . . Are the trees your enemies, that you should attack them?*

Even in time of war, God is concerned about the needless destruction of the environment.

LEVITICUS 25:4-5 | *During the seventh year the land must have a . . . year of complete rest.*

God's instructions for the people of Israel to let farmland rest every seventh year allowed for the conservation of good, productive land.

PSALM 96:11-13 | *Let the heavens be glad, and the earth rejoice! Let the sea and everything in it shout his praise! Let the fields and their crops burst out with joy! Let the trees of the forest rustle with praise before the LORD, for he is coming!*

God created nature to proclaim his glory. You should do all you can to preserve this testimony for God.

Promise from God PSALM 19:1-2, 4 | *The heavens proclaim the glory of God. The skies display his craftsmanship. Day after day they continue to speak; night after night they make him known. . . . Their message has gone throughout the earth, and their words to all the world.*

EXAMPLE

In what ways can I be a good example?

JEREMIAH 1:10 | *[The Lord said,] "Today I appoint you to stand up against nations and kingdoms."*

A good role model not only does what is right but speaks out against wrong.

1 THESSALONIANS 1:5 | *You know of our concern for you from the way we lived when we were with you.*

A good role model is responsible and accountable and shows his or her faith by actions.

HEBREWS 5:12 | *You have been believers so long now that you ought to be teaching others.*

A good role model teaches others about God's ways.

MATTHEW 5:13 | *You are the salt of the earth. But what good is salt if it has lost its flavor?*

TITUS 2:7 | *You . . . must be an example . . . by doing good works of every kind. Let everything you do reflect the integrity and seriousness of your teaching.*

A good role model is not influenced by evil but rather does good to others and also influences others for good.

HOSEA 6:3 | *Oh, that we might know the LORD! Let us press on to know him.*

Being a good role model doesn't mean that you are perfect but that you are striving for maturity.

MATTHEW 20:28 | *Even the Son of Man came not to be served but to serve others and to give his life as a ransom for many.*

Being a good role model doesn't make you a celebrity; it makes you a servant.

1 TIMOTHY 4:12 | *Don't let anyone think less of you because you are young. Be an example to all believers in what you say, in the way you live, in your love, your faith, and your purity.*

Age need not be a barrier to being a good role model.

Who is the ultimate role model?

1 CORINTHIANS 11:1 | *You should imitate me, just as I imitate Christ.*

In other people you find assorted characteristics you would like to develop in your own life. In Jesus Christ are all the characteristics you should imitate. When you have a question about what to do, ask what Jesus would do.

Promise from God HEBREWS 12:12-13 | *Take a new grip with your tired hands and strengthen your weak knees. Mark out a straight path for your feet so that those who are weak and lame will not fall but become strong.*

EXCELLENCE

Where did excellence of workmanship have its origin?

GENESIS 1:31 | *God looked over all he had made, and he saw that it was very good!*

PSALM 19:1 | *The heavens proclaim the glory of God. The skies display his craftsmanship.*

The splendor of pristine creation—nature, animals, and people—was excellence in its purest form. Not only was the end product excellent, but it was excellent in every detail. The glory of the Creator was reflected in the excellence of his creation.

ISAIAH 35:2 | *Yes, there will be an abundance of flowers and singing and joy! The deserts will become as green as the mountains of Lebanon, as lovely as Mount Carmel or the plain of Sharon. There the LORD will display his glory, the splendor of our God.*

All nature sings and displays a beauty of symmetry that surpasses all the finest musical, poetic, or artistic genius of all people anytime, anywhere.

Why is excellence encouraged by God? Why should I strive to be excellent?

EXODUS 35:31-33 | *The LORD has filled Bezalel with the Spirit of God, giving him great wisdom, ability, and expertise in all kinds of crafts. He is a master craftsman. . . . He is skilled. . . . He is a master at every craft.*

God places great value on excellence and, therefore, created you with unique and special gifts to help you become excellent in some area.

1 CHRONICLES 26:6 | *Shemaiah had sons with great ability who earned positions of great authority.*

Excellence is highly valued. Those who strive for excellence are often promoted to significant positions in order to impact a greater number of people.

2 CHRONICLES 30:21-22, 26 | *Each day the Levites and priests sang to the LORD, accompanied by loud instruments. Hezekiah*

encouraged all the Levites regarding the skill they displayed. . . .
There was great joy in the city, for Jerusalem had not seen
a celebration like this one since the days of Solomon, King
David's son.

Excellence is appreciated. It inspires, satisfies, blesses, and
motivates others.

NEHEMIAH 13:13 | *These men had an excellent reputation, and it*
was their job to make honest distributions to their fellow Levites.

Excellence usually enhances your reputation. It would be
tragic if you were remembered as valuing mediocrity.

EPHESIANS 4:11-12 | *These are the gifts Christ gave to the church*
. . . to equip God's people to do his work and build up the
church, the body of Christ.

Excellence engages and challenges you; it urges you to make
a unique contribution.

1 PETER 4:11 | *Do you have the gift of helping others? Do it with*
all the strength and energy that God supplies.

Excellence is helpful to others. For example, doctors who
strive for excellence have a better chance of helping others
get well. Parents who work hard at raising their children
will give them essential tools to better equip them for the
real world.

PSALM 98:5 | *Sing your praise to the LORD with the harp, with*
the harp and melodious song.

Pursuing excellence is an act of worship.

2 CORINTHIANS 3:18 | *The Lord—who is the Spirit—makes us more*
and more like him as we are changed into his glorious image.

Excellence is an indication that we are striving to be like Christ, who was and is excellent in every way.

Promise from God COLOSSIANS 3:23-24 | *Work willingly at whatever you do, as though you were working for the Lord rather than for people. Remember that the Lord will give you an inheritance as your reward, and that the Master you are serving is Christ.*

EXCUSES

What is the first excuse in the Bible?

GENESIS 3:11-12 | *[The Lord God asked,] "Have you eaten from the tree whose fruit I commanded you not to eat?" The man replied, "It was the woman you gave me who gave me the fruit, and I ate it."*

Adam, the first man, made the first excuse. He ate the fruit, but he blamed Eve for offering it to him and indirectly blamed God because God had given him "the woman." Then Eve blamed the serpent for convincing her to eat the fruit (see Genesis 3:13). Both tried to excuse their actions by blaming someone else. It is interesting that people started making excuses after the very first sin!

What are some examples of other people who had poor excuses?

EXODUS 32:24 | *[Aaron said to Moses,] "So I told [the people], 'Whoever has gold jewelry, take it off.' When they brought it to me, I simply threw it into the fire—and out came this calf!"*

Aaron's lame excuse for making an idol—something expressly condemned by God—was that it just happened! How often do you do the same thing, blaming your intentional sin on circumstances beyond your control?

1 SAMUEL 15:1, 3, 9, 15 | *[Samuel said to Saul,] "Listen to this message from the LORD! . . . Go and completely destroy the entire Amalekite nation." . . . [But] Saul and his men . . . kept the best. . . . "It's true that the army spared the best of the sheep, goats, and cattle," Saul admitted. "But they are going to sacrifice them to the LORD your God. We have destroyed everything else."*

Saul tried to justify his sinful actions with the excuse that he sinned in order to do a good thing. His life was a story of one excuse after another. Finally he ran out of excuses and lost his kingdom because he simply wouldn't own up to his mistakes and admit that he was wrong (see 1 Samuel 15:26).

LUKE 22:60 | *Peter said, "Man, I don't know what you are talking about."*

Peter had an excuse for pretending he did not know Jesus—he wanted to save his life or at least avoid the ridicule of being associated with Jesus. Ironically, it is when you start making excuses about knowing Jesus that you are in the greatest danger of losing all that he offers.

Can I ever excuse myself from God's work because I lack abilities or resources?

EXODUS 4:10 | *Moses pleaded with the LORD, "O Lord, I'm not very good with words. I never have been, and I'm not now, even though you have spoken to me. I get tongue-tied, and my words get tangled."*

JUDGES 6:15-16 | *"But Lord," Gideon replied, "how can I rescue Israel? My clan is the weakest in the whole tribe of Manasseh, and I am the least in my entire family!" The LORD said to him, "I will be with you."*

Both Moses and Gideon thought they had a good excuse to get out of serving God. But the qualifications God looks for are different from what we might expect. He often chooses the least likely people to do his work in order to more effectively demonstrate his power. If you know God has called you to do something, stop trying to excuse yourself. He will give you the help and strength you need to get the job done.

Can I be excused for not accepting the Lord?

PHILIPPIANS 2:10-11 | *At the name of Jesus every knee should bow . . . and every tongue confess that Jesus Christ is Lord, to the glory of God the Father.*

You may have all kinds of excuses for avoiding God—being too busy, blaming God for your hardships, procrastinating, not wanting to give up your favorite vices, or even not knowing where to begin. Do you think any of those excuses will hold up when you see God face-to-face?

ROMANS 1:20 | *Ever since the world was created, people have seen the earth and sky. Through everything God made, they can clearly see his invisible qualities—his eternal power and divine nature. So they have no excuse for not knowing God.*

Everyone has seen the testimony of nature, God's work, which the Bible says clearly reveals the hand of an almighty Creator. That alone witnesses to his presence and power. If you fail to come to terms with God, you are really without excuse.

Promise from God 1 PETER 1:17 | *Remember that the heavenly Father to whom you pray has no favorites. He will judge or reward you according to what you do.*

FAILURE

What is failure in God's eyes?

EXODUS 34:6-7 | *The LORD passed in front of Moses, calling out, "Yahweh! The LORD! The God of compassion and mercy! I am slow to anger and filled with unfailing love and faithfulness. I lavish unfailing love to a thousand generations. I forgive iniquity, rebellion, and sin. But I do not excuse the guilty."*

MALACHI 3:5 | *"At that time I will put you on trial. . . . I will speak against those who cheat employees of their wages, who oppress widows and orphans, or who deprive the foreigners living among you of justice, for these people do not fear me," says the LORD of Heaven's Armies.*

Failure in God's eyes is living contrary to the way he created you to live. God gave you the gift of life and created you to have a relationship with him. Your greatest failure would be to reject that way of life and to reject the God who gave you life.

What must I learn about failure?

GENESIS 3:12-13 | *[Adam said to God], "It was the woman you gave me who gave me the fruit, and I ate it." . . . "The serpent deceived me," [Eve] replied.*

2 CORINTHIANS 12:9 | *[God] said, "My grace is all you need. My power works best in weakness."*

One thing is certain: You must learn to live with failure. Everyone has weaknesses. The key to character is not how little you fail, but how you respond to failure. Adam and Eve, for example, responded to their failures by trying to blame each other rather than admitting their mistakes and seeking forgiveness.

JONAH 1:3 | *Jonah . . . went in the opposite direction to get away from the LORD.*

Don't make the mistake of running from God. That is the worst kind of failure and will bring the worst kind of consequences.

GENESIS 4:6-7 | *"Why are you so angry?" the LORD asked Cain. "Why do you look so dejected? You will be accepted if you do what is right. But if you refuse to do what is right, then watch out! Sin is crouching at the door, eager to control you. But you must subdue it and be its master."*

PROVERBS 29:1 | *Whoever stubbornly refuses to accept criticism will suddenly be destroyed beyond recovery.*

If you are told you have made a mistake, you must consider the source and the substance of the criticism, then reflect and learn for the future.

MATTHEW 26:74 | *Peter swore, "A curse on me if I'm lying—I don't know the man!"*

Following Jesus means allowing him to forgive your failures so you can move on and experience joy and success. Jesus restored Peter to fellowship and service even after his most painful failure.

What are some ways I can prevent failure?

PROVERBS 15:22 | *Plans go wrong for lack of advice; many advisers bring success.*

Good advice helps prevent failure. A concert of wise counsel makes good music for your success.

MATTHEW 16:26 | *What do you benefit if you gain the whole world but lose your own soul? Is anything worth more than your soul?*

If you managed a successful business, raised a good family, won all kinds of community awards, and retired comfortably, would you say life had been a success? God says you would have failed if you had done all of this apart from him. Life apart from God now means life apart from him for eternity. Don't fail by neglecting or ignoring God. Don't fail to discover what a relationship with God means for your future.

When I have failed, how do I get past the failure? How can I turn it into success?

1 JOHN 2:1-2 | *My dear children, I am writing this to you so that you will not sin. But if anyone does sin, we have an advocate who pleads our case before the Father. He is Jesus Christ,*

the one who is truly righteous. He himself is the sacrifice that atones for our sins—and not only our sins but the sins of all the world.

Your failure doesn't surprise God. God gave his Son, Jesus Christ, to pay the debt of your failure and bring you back into full fellowship with him. The wonder of the gospel is that your failure reveals God's greatest success.

MICAH 7:8 | *Though I fall, I will rise again. Though I sit in darkness, the LORD will be my light.*

2 CORINTHIANS 4:9 | *We are hunted down, but never abandoned by God. We get knocked down, but we are not destroyed.*

When you fail, you must get up again. Do not be afraid of failing. Many of life's inspiring success stories come from people who failed many times but never gave up. Most important, never give up on your relationship with God, who promises you ultimate victory through eternal life.

1 CORINTHIANS 10:6 | *These things happened as a warning to us.*

Remember that failure can be helpful: It can teach you important lessons about what to avoid in the future. You need not repeat your own mistakes or copy the mistakes you recognize in others!

HEBREWS 4:15-16 | *This High Priest of ours understands our weaknesses. . . . So let us come boldly to the throne of our gracious God . . . [to] find grace to help us when we need it most.*

Realize that God's work is not limited by your failures. He does not reject you in your weakness but rather embraces you so that you can receive strength to be all he intends you to be. When failure drives you into the arms of God, then your failure is truly a success.

Promise from God 2 CORINTHIANS 12:9 | *[God] said, "My grace is all you need. My power works best in weakness."*

FAITH

Why should I have faith in God?

JOHN 3:16 | *God loved the world so much that he gave his one and only Son, so that everyone who believes in him will not perish but have eternal life.*

JOHN 5:24 | *[Jesus said,] "I tell you the truth, those who listen to my message and believe in God who sent me have eternal life."*

According to the Bible (God's own words), faith in God means believing that he sent his Son, Jesus Christ, to earth to save you from eternal death. Believing that Jesus died for your sins and rose again from the dead is the only way to receive the gift of eternal life in heaven. The One who created heaven has told you clearly how to get there.

HEBREWS 11:1 | *Faith is the confidence that what we hope for will actually happen; it gives us assurance about things we cannot see.*

Faith gives you hope. When the world seems to be a crazy, mixed-up place, you can be absolutely confident that one day Jesus will come and make it right again. Your faith in his promise to do that someday will allow you to keep going today.

Faith seems so complicated; how can I ever "get it"?

MARK 5:36 | *Jesus . . . said to Jairus, "Don't be afraid. Just have faith."*

Too often we make faith too complicated. It simply means trusting Jesus to do what he has promised—and he promised to give you life forever in heaven if you just believe he is who he said he is, the Son of God.

How much faith must I have?

MATTHEW 17:20 | *[Jesus said,] "I tell you the truth, if you had faith even as small as a mustard seed, you could say to this mountain, 'Move from here to there,' and it would move. Nothing would be impossible."*

The mustard seed was often used to illustrate the smallest seed known to people. Jesus said that it is not the size of your faith but the size of the One in whom you believe that makes the difference. You do not have to have great faith in God; rather you have faith in a great God.

How can I strengthen my faith?

GENESIS 12:1, 4 | *The LORD had said to Abram, "Leave your native country . . . and go to the land that I will show you. . . . So Abram departed as the LORD had instructed.*

Like a muscle, faith gets stronger the more you exercise it. When you do what God asks you to do and then see him bless you as a result of your obedience, your faith grows.

PSALM 119:48 | *I honor and love your commands. I meditate on your decrees.*

ROMANS 10:17 | *Faith comes from hearing . . . the Good News about Christ.*

Faith is grounded in God's Word. Your faith will grow stronger as you study the Bible and reflect on the truths about who God is, his guidelines for your life, and how he wants to do his work on earth through you.

2 KINGS 6:17 | *Elisha prayed, "O LORD, open his eyes and let him see!" The LORD opened the young man's eyes, and when he looked up, he saw that the hillside around Elisha was filled with horses and chariots of fire.*

JOHN 20:27-29 | *[Jesus] said to Thomas, "Put your finger here, and look at my hands. Put your hand into the wound in my side. Don't be faithless any longer. Believe!" "My Lord and my God!" Thomas exclaimed. Then Jesus told him, "You believe because you have seen me. Blessed are those who believe without seeing me."*

2 CORINTHIANS 3:14 | *The people's minds were hardened, and to this day whenever the old covenant is being read, the same veil covers their minds so they cannot understand the truth. And this veil can be removed only by believing in Christ.*

The strongest faith is not one based on physical senses but on spiritual conviction. There is a spiritual element to this world that you cannot see, but it is very real. Your faith will become stronger the more you allow the Holy Spirit to strengthen your "spiritual vision"; then you will sense and see the results of God working in your life and in the lives of those around you.

Promise from God ACTS 16:31 | *Believe in the Lord Jesus and you will be saved.*

FEAR

What can I do when I am overcome with fear?

PSALM 46:1-2 | *God is our refuge and strength, always ready to help in times of trouble. So we will not fear when earthquakes come and the mountains crumble into the sea.*

Remind yourself that God is greater than the most severe threats in life. You will not be surprised or overcome by trouble if you recognize how sin has corrupted this world and if you remember he promises to always be ready to help when you ask.

DEUTERONOMY 31:6 | *Be strong and courageous! Do not be afraid and do not panic . . . for the LORD your God will personally go ahead of you. He will neither fail you nor abandon you.*

JOHN 14:27 | *[Jesus said,] "I am leaving you with a gift—peace of mind and heart. And the peace I give is a gift the world cannot give. So don't be troubled or afraid."*

Remind yourself that God is always with you. Your situation may be genuinely threatening, but God has not abandoned you and he promises to stay with you. Even if your situation is so bad that it results in death, God has not left you but has instead ushered you into his very presence.

EPHESIANS 1:3 | *All praise to God, the Father of our Lord Jesus Christ, who has blessed us with every spiritual blessing in the heavenly realms because we are united with Christ.*

Remind yourself that no enemy or adversity can take away your most important blessings—God's forgiveness for your sins, your relationship with him, and your eternal salvation. These remain secure even when your world falls apart.

2 TIMOTHY 1:7 | *God has not given us a spirit of fear and timidity, but of power, love, and self-discipline.*

Whatever makes you afraid is an opportunity for you to develop greater faith as you call upon the power of God to help you.

GENESIS 26:7 | *He was afraid to say, "She is my wife." He thought, "They will kill me to get her."*

JOSHUA 17:16 | *The Canaanites . . . have iron chariots. . . . They are too strong for us.*

Fear must not keep you from doing the things you know are right. You are not meant to live in fear.

What does it mean to fear God?

PSALM 33:8 | *Let the whole world fear the LORD, and let everyone stand in awe of him.*

PROVERBS 9:10 | *Fear of the LORD is the foundation of wisdom.*

Fearing God is not the same as being afraid of God. Being afraid of someone drives you away from him or her. Fearing God means being awed by his power and goodness. This draws you closer to him and to the blessings he gives. A healthy fear should drive you to God for forgiveness and help you keep your perspective about where you need to be in your relationship with him.

How can fearing God make you joyful?

PSALM 2:11 | *Serve the LORD with reverent fear, and rejoice with trembling.*

PSALM 128:1 | *How joyful are those who fear the LORD— all who follow his ways!*

A healthy fear of God recognizes what he could do if he gave you what you deserved. But rejoice, instead, that he gives you mercy and forgiveness. You fear God because of his awesome power; you love God for the way he blesses you with it. And this brings great joy.

Promise from God ISAIAH 41:10 | *Don't be afraid, for I am with you. Don't be discouraged, for I am your God. I will strengthen you and help you. I will hold you up with my victorious right hand.*

FORGIVENESS

What does it really mean to be forgiven?

ISAIAH 1:18 | *The LORD [said,] "Though your sins are like scarlet, I will make them as white as snow. Though they are red like crimson, I will make them as white as wool."*

COLOSSIANS 1:22 | *You are holy and blameless as you stand before him without a single fault.*

Forgiveness means that God looks at you as though you had never sinned. When you receive his forgiveness, you are blameless before him. When God forgives, he doesn't sweep your sins under the carpet; instead, he completely washes them away.

MATTHEW 5:44 | *Love your enemies! Pray for those who perse-cute you!*

Forgiveness paves the way for harmonious relationships, even with your enemies.

COLOSSIANS 2:13 | *You were dead because of your sins and because your sinful nature was not yet cut away. Then God made you alive with Christ, for he forgave all our sins.*

Forgiveness brings great joy because you are no longer a captive to your sinful nature.

ACTS 2:38 | *Each of you must repent of your sins and turn to God, and be baptized in the name of Jesus Christ for the forgiveness of your sins. Then you will receive the gift of the Holy Spirit.*

Forgiveness of sins allows you to receive the gift of God's Holy Spirit. The Holy Spirit allows you to tap into the very power of God to help you battle temptation and to guide you through life.

How do I receive God's loving forgiveness?

2 CHRONICLES 7:14 | *If my people . . . will humble themselves and pray and seek my face and turn from their wicked ways, I will hear from heaven and will forgive their sins.*

1 JOHN 1:9 | *If we confess our sins to him, he is faithful and just to forgive us.*

Confessing sin is the first step to forgiveness. After you ask for forgiveness, you simply have to accept the gift of forgiveness. Receiving God's forgiveness is the only way you can have the assurance of eternal life in heaven.

Can any sin be forgiven? There must be some sin too great to be forgiven.

JOEL 2:32 | *Everyone who calls on the name of the LORD will be saved.*

MARK 3:28 | *[Jesus said,] "I tell you the truth, all sin . . . can be forgiven."*

ROMANS 8:38 | *Nothing can ever separate us from God's love.*

Forgiveness is not based on the magnitude of the sin but on the magnitude of the forgiver's love. No sin is too great for God's complete and unconditional love. The Bible does actually mention one unforgivable sin—an attitude of defiant hostility toward God that prevents us from accepting his forgiveness. Those who don't want his forgiveness are out of its reach.

How can I forgive someone who has hurt me deeply?

MATTHEW 6:14-15 | *If you forgive those who sin against you, your heavenly Father will forgive you. But if you refuse to forgive others, your Father will not forgive your sins.*

Being unwilling to forgive shows that you have not understood or benefited from God's forgiveness.

MATTHEW 5:44 | *Love your enemies! Pray for those who persecute you!*

Pray for those who hate and hurt you. This releases you from the destructive emotions of anger, bitterness, and revenge and helps you to forgive those who have hurt you.

LUKE 23:34 | *Jesus said, "Father, forgive them, for they don't know what they are doing."*

Jesus forgave even those who mocked and killed him. Be more concerned about your offenders and their relationship with God and less about nursing your own grudges and self-pity.

1 PETER 3:9 | *Don't repay evil for evil. Don't retaliate with insults when people insult you. Instead, pay them back with a blessing. That is what God has called you to do, and he will bless you for it.*

When people say hurtful things about you, God wants you to respond by blessing them.

EPHESIANS 4:31 | *Get rid of all bitterness, rage, anger, harsh words, and slander, as well as all types of evil behavior.*

An unforgiving attitude not only ruins your relationships but also poisons your soul. The person most hurt by unforgiveness is you.

Promise from God ISAIAH 43:25 | *I—yes, I alone— will blot out your sins for my own sake and will never think of them again.*

FRIENDSHIP

What is the mark of true friendship?

1 SAMUEL 18:1, 3-4 | *After David had finished talking with Saul, he met Jonathan, the king's son. There was an immediate bond between them. . . . Jonathan made a solemn pact with David, because he loved him as he loved himself. Jonathan sealed the pact by taking off his robe and giving it to David, together with his tunic, sword, bow, and belt.*

PROVERBS 17:17 | *A friend is always loyal, and a brother is born to help in time of need.*

Some friendships are fleeting and some are lasting. True friendships are glued together with bonds of loyalty and commitment. They remain intact, despite changing external circumstances.

What gets in the way of friendships?

1 SAMUEL 18:8-11 | *Saul [was] very angry. "What's this?" he said. "They credit David with ten thousands and me with only thousands. Next they'll be making him their king!" So from that time on Saul kept a jealous eye on David. The very next day . . . David was playing the harp. . . . Saul had a spear in his hand, and he suddenly hurled it at David, intending to pin him to the wall.*

Jealousy is the great dividing force of friendships. Envy over what a friend has will soon turn to anger and bitterness, causing you to separate yourself from the one you truly cared for.

PSALM 41:9 | *Even my best friend, the one I trusted completely, . . . has turned against me.*

When respect and trust are seriously damaged, even the closest friendship is at risk.

2 SAMUEL 13:11 | *As she was feeding him, he grabbed her and demanded, "Come to bed with me."*

Friendships are destroyed when boundaries are violated.

Male/female friendships involve unique pressures and temptations. Does the Bible offer any guidelines for male/female friendships?

1 CORINTHIANS 13:4-5, 7 | *Love is patient and kind. Love is not jealous. . . . It does not demand its own way. . . . Love never gives up, never loses faith, is always hopeful, and endures through every circumstance.*

This timeless description of Christian love becomes the standard of respect and conduct that should mark all relationships.

1 TIMOTHY 5:1-2 | *Talk to younger men as you would to your own brothers. . . . Treat younger women with all purity as you would your own sisters.*

Opposite-sex friendships are valuable, especially since it's important that the person you marry be your friend. As a Christian, you have a responsibility to encourage your friends to grow closer to Christ regardless of their gender. The best way to keep your friendships pure is to treat your friends like brothers and sisters. Paul gave women such as Lydia and

Priscilla this kind of respect. You can do the same by training yourself to focus on your friends' hearts—who they really are.

MATTHEW 5:28 | *Anyone who even looks at a woman with lust has already committed adultery with her in his heart.*

EPHESIANS 5:3, 18 | *Let there be no sexual immorality, impurity, or greed among you. . . . Be filled with the Holy Spirit.*

In dramatic contrast to much that you see in today's culture, Jesus calls you to a standard of sexual purity in thought as well as in action.

Can I truly be friends with God?

EXODUS 33:11 | *The LORD would speak to Moses face to face, as one speaks to a friend.*

PSALM 25:14 | *The LORD is a friend to those who fear him. He teaches them his covenant.*

God saw Moses as his friend. As you develop your relationship with God, you develop a friendship with him. He is your Lord, but he also desires to be your friend.

Promise from God LEVITICUS 26:12 | *I will walk among you; I will be your God.*

FRUSTRATION

How should I respond to frustration?

GENESIS 3:17-19 | *The ground is cursed because of you. All your life you will struggle to scratch a living from it. It will grow*

thorns and thistles for you, though you will eat of its grains.
By the sweat of your brow will you have food to eat.

Frustration is ultimately the consequence of the curse of sin—things just don't go the way you want them to. While you don't welcome frustration, you shouldn't be surprised by it. You live in a fallen world, with fallen people; therefore you can expect obstacles and resistance in all forms. When you realize and accept frustration as a part of everyday life, you are better prepared to handle it in a positive way.

PROVERBS 21:2 | *People may be right in their own eyes, but the LORD examines their heart.*

Examining the source of your frustration helps you know how to deal with it. There is a big difference between being frustrated in your quest to do good and being frustrated because you are not getting your way. Each frustration must be dealt with individually.

EXODUS 17:4 | *Moses cried out to the LORD, "What should I do with these people?"*

JOHN 6:7 | *Philip [said], "Even if we worked for months, we wouldn't have enough money to feed them!"*

Recognize that many of your problems don't have a human solution. You must take them to God.

JOSHUA 1:9 | *Be strong and courageous! Do not be afraid or discouraged. For the LORD your God is with you wherever you go.*

Don't be discouraged. God will give you strength and courage to see you through.

What frustrates God?

PSALM 78:40-42 | *Oh, how often they rebelled against him in the wilderness and grieved his heart in that dry wasteland. Again and again they tested God's patience and provoked the Holy One of Israel. They did not remember his power and how he rescued them from their enemies.*

HOSEA 6:4 | *"O Israel and Judah, what should I do with you?" asks the LORD. "For your love vanishes like the morning mist and disappears like dew in the sunlight."*

It is frustrating to God to give unending love, mercy, and forgiveness to his people, only to see them block these blessings and starve their souls in a spiritual desert.

Promise from God 1 CHRONICLES 28:20 | *Be strong and courageous, and do the work. Don't be afraid or discouraged, for the LORD God, my God, is with you. . . . He will see to it that all the work . . . is finished correctly.*

GIVING

Why should I give?

LUKE 21:3 | *"I tell you the truth," Jesus said, "this poor widow has given more than all the rest of [the rich people]."*

JOHN 3:16 | *God loved the world so much that he gave his one and only Son.*

You should give to model, and learn the power of, the sacrificial giving of God.

EXODUS 23:19 | *As you harvest your crops, bring the very best of the first harvest to the house of the LORD your God.*

You should give first to God because it demonstrates that he is first in your life.

1 CHRONICLES 29:14 | *Everything we have has come from you, and we give you only what you first gave us!*

You should give because it reminds you that what you own is a gift from God.

PSALM 54:6 | *I will sacrifice a voluntary offering to you.*

You should give because it develops a habit of thankfulness. The more you give, the more you are grateful for what you have.

2 CORINTHIANS 9:11 | *When we take your gifts to those who need them, they will thank God.*

You should give to others so that God will be glorified.

1 PETER 4:10 | *God has given each of you a gift from his great variety of spiritual gifts. Use them well to serve one another.*

The more you give of yourself, the more God's generosity flows through you.

2 CORINTHIANS 9:6 | *Remember this—a farmer who plants only a few seeds will get a small crop. But the one who plants generously will get a generous crop.*

You should not give in order to get more, but your resources often grow as you give more. One of the reasons this occurs is that the qualities that make you generous also make you responsible and trustworthy. But another important reason is that God, in his grace, may entrust more to you so that you will be a bigger channel of his blessing in this world.

How much should I give?

DEUTERONOMY 14:22 | *You must set aside a tithe of your crops—one-tenth of all the crops you harvest each year.*

1 CORINTHIANS 16:2 | *On the first day of each week, you should each put aside a portion of the money you have earned.*

2 CORINTHIANS 9:7 | *You must each decide in your heart how much to give. And don't give reluctantly or in response to pressure. "For God loves a person who gives cheerfully."*

While the Old Testament specifically talks about giving one-tenth of what you earn to God, the New Testament encourages you to give what you can, to give sacrificially, and to give with a grateful and generous heart. For many, this will mean giving far more than one-tenth!

But I'm just barely making it with my budget. What if I don't seem to have enough to give?

PROVERBS 28:27 | *Whoever gives to the poor will lack nothing.*

MALACHI 3:10 | *"Bring all the tithes into the storehouse so there will be enough food in my Temple. If you do," says the LORD of Heaven's Armies, "I will open the windows of heaven for you. I will pour out a blessing so great you won't have enough room to take it in! Try it! Put me to the test!"*

God promises to provide for you when you give back to him.

2 CORINTHIANS 9:8 | *God will generously provide all you need. Then you will always have everything you need and plenty left over to share with others.*

It's easy to think you would be happy if you had just a little more. The secrets of happiness, however, are learning to be content with what you have, whether it is much or little, and learning to live abundantly even with little.

Promise from God LUKE 6:38 | *Give, and you will receive. Your gift will return to you in full—pressed down, shaken together to make room for more, running over, and poured into your lap. The amount you give will determine the amount you get back.*

GOSSIP

Why is gossip so bad?

JAMES 1:26 | *If you claim to be religious but don't control your tongue, you are fooling yourself, and your religion is worthless.*

What comes out of your mouth shows what is in your heart. Gossip, criticism, flattery, lies, and profanity are not only "word" problems but "heart" problems as well.

PROVERBS 11:13 | *A gossip goes around telling secrets, but those who are trustworthy can keep a confidence.*

Gossips make poor friends. Gossips are demolition experts, trying to tear others down, while trustworthy people build others up.

ROMANS 1:29 | *Their lives became full of every kind of wickedness, sin, greed, hate, envy, murder, quarreling, deception, malicious behavior, and gossip.*

God catalogs gossip with such sins as greed, hate, envy, and murder.

1 TIMOTHY 5:13 | *If they are on the list [for support], [the younger widows] will learn to be lazy and will spend their time gossiping from house to house, meddling in other people's business and talking about things they shouldn't.*

Gossiping often grows out of idleness. If you have nothing better to do than sit around talking about other people, you wind up saying things you later regret.

PROVERBS 18:8 | *Rumors are dainty morsels that sink deep into one's heart.*

Gossip hurts others. It also destroys your credibility if the gossip proves false.

How do I stop gossip?

PROVERBS 26:20 | *Fire goes out without wood, and quarrels disappear when gossip stops.*

Stop the chain of gossip with you! When you hear gossip, you can do something about it—you can decide not to spread it any further.

DEUTERONOMY 13:14 | *You must examine the facts carefully.*

If you are concerned about something you've heard, you must look carefully into the matter without assuming what you have been told is true. Go to the source and get the facts straight.

MATTHEW 7:12 | *Do to others whatever you would like them to do to you.*

The Golden Rule can also be applied to your speech—"Talk about others in the same way you would like them to talk about you."

EPHESIANS 4:29 | *Let everything you say be good and helpful, so that your words will be an encouragement to those who hear them.*

It's really true—what you spend most of your time thinking about is what you end up doing. When you're tempted to complain, train yourself instead to pray. When you're tempted to gossip, compliment or encourage someone instead.

COLOSSIANS 3:17 | *Whatever you do or say, do it as a representative of the Lord Jesus.*

If you think you may be about to gossip, ask yourself, "Does the person I'm talking to need to know this? Is it true, accurate, and helpful?"

Promise from God 1 PETER 3:10 | *If you want to enjoy life and see many happy days, keep your tongue from speaking evil and your lips from telling lies.*

GRACE

What is grace?

ROMANS 6:23 | *The wages of sin is death, but the free gift of God is eternal life through Christ Jesus our Lord.*

EPHESIANS 2:8-9 | *God saved you by his grace when you believed. And you can't take credit for this; it is a gift from God. Salvation is not a reward for the good things we have done, so none of us can boast about it.*

Grace is a big favor done for someone without expecting anything in return. When the Bible says you are saved by grace, it means that God has done you the biggest favor of all—he has pardoned you from the death sentence you deserve for rebelling against him. By grace, you are forgiven for your sin and restored to full fellowship with God. Like the gift of life itself, you cannot take credit for it—any more than a baby can brag about being born! The only hitch to grace is that you must accept it as a gift; otherwise you can't enjoy its benefits.

How do I receive God's grace?

PSALM 84:11 | *The LORD God . . . gives us grace and glory. The LORD will withhold no good thing from those who do what is right.*

Grace begins with God and is given freely by God. You simply accept it as a gift. Then his graciousness to you is your example for extending grace and mercy to others.

EPHESIANS 2:8 | *God saved you by his grace when you believed. And you can't take credit for this; it is a gift from God.*

It is by God's grace that he decided to offer the gift of salvation. There is nothing you can do to earn it. You simply receive it with faith and thankfulness.

HEBREWS 4:16 | *Let us come boldly to the throne of our gracious God. There we will receive his mercy, and we will find grace to help us when we need it most.*

You may freely approach God at any time, and he will freely give his mercy and grace.

How does grace affect my daily life?

ROMANS 6:14 | *Sin is no longer your master, for you no longer live under the requirements of the law. Instead, you live under the freedom of God's grace.*

God's grace provides forgiveness for your sin and breaks its power over your life. The Holy Spirit gives you a desire to want to please God and the spiritual wisdom to be able to discern the truth and pursue it.

GALATIANS 3:3 | *How foolish can you be? After starting your Christian lives in the Spirit, why are you now trying to become perfect by your own human effort?*

You need to continually remind yourself that God's approval of you is because of his grace alone. God approves of you not because of what you do or don't do, but because he loves you and has forgiven all your sins.

How does grace affect my view of God?

PSALM 103:8 | *The LORD is compassionate and merciful, slow to get angry and filled with unfailing love.*

If you believe God is always angry with you, you will be defensive, fearful, or antagonistic toward him. When you understand the depth of his love and grace toward you, you live with the joy of being forgiven and the knowledge that you will live forever in heaven. You no longer fear God's retribution but pursue a relationship with him.

Promise from God   ROMANS 6:14 | *Sin is no longer your master. . . . Instead, you live under the freedom of God's grace.*

GREED

What can greed do to me?

ISAIAH 56:11 | *They are never satisfied . . . , all following their own path and intent on personal gain.*

Greed can so consume you that you become blind to others' needs. It lives at the opposite end of the spectrum from generosity, giving, and graciousness.

EXODUS 20:17 | *You must not covet your neighbor's house. You must not covet your neighbor's wife . . . or anything else that belongs to your neighbor.*

Envying and coveting are forms of greed. Greed is dangerous because, left unchecked, it can grow to be so powerful that it will control your life, causing you to be obsessed with something you want, even if it is something you know you should not have.

2 CHRONICLES 10:14-15 | *[Rehoboam] told the people, "My father laid heavy burdens on you, but I'm going to make them even heavier!" . . . So the king paid no attention to the people.*

PROVERBS 11:24 | *Give freely and become more wealthy; be stingy and lose everything.*

Motivated to get more for himself, Rehoboam pressed his people to the breaking point and lost half his kingdom (see 2 Chronicles 10:16-19). The more obsessed you are with having more, the greater the odds that you will wind up with less.

How can I resist the temptation to be greedy?

MARK 10:21-22 | *Looking at the man, Jesus felt genuine love for him. "There is still one thing you haven't done," he told him. "Go and sell all your possessions and give the money to the poor, and you will have treasure in heaven. Then come, follow me." At this the man's face fell, and he went away sad, for he had many possessions.*

Ask yourself, *How tightly do I hold on to what I have?* Jesus doesn't ask most of us to give up everything we have, but if he did, could you?

1 SAMUEL 8:3 | *They were greedy for money. They accepted bribes and perverted justice.*

Ask yourself, *Do I know anyone who is greedy and stingy? Do I really want to become like that person?*

MATTHEW 6:19-21 | *Don't store up treasures here on earth. . . . Store your treasures in heaven. . . . Wherever your treasure is, there the desires of your heart will also be.*

Ask yourself, *How long do I want to enjoy the good things in life?* If you want to enjoy them temporarily, just in this life, you will have more trouble with greed. If you want to enjoy them for eternity, you will invest in different things now so that you can enjoy God's rewards forever.

JOB 1:21 | *I came naked from my mother's womb, and I will be naked when I leave. The LORD gave me what I had, and the LORD has taken it away. Praise the name of the LORD!*

1 CORINTHIANS 4:7 | *What do you have that God hasn't given you? And if everything you have is from God, why boast as though it were not a gift?*

Ask yourself, *Who really owns my things?* Remind yourself that everything comes from the hand of God, and therefore everything is God's. This changes your perspective on your possessions.

COLOSSIANS 3:2-3 | *Think about the things of heaven, not the things of earth. For you died to this life, and your real life is hidden with Christ in God.*

Ask yourself, *What do I think about most?* Redirect your focus from material things that don't last to things that last forever—your relationship with God and with others.

Promise from God MATTHEW 6:19-21 | *Don't store up treasures here on earth. . . . Store your treasures in heaven, where moths and rust cannot destroy, and thieves do not break in and steal. Wherever your treasure is, there the desires of your heart will also be.*

GRIEF

What might cause me to grieve?

RUTH 1:9 | *She kissed them good-bye, and they all broke down and wept.*

You grieve when you have to say good-bye to people you love.

JOHN 11:13, 35 | *Lazarus had died. . . . Then Jesus wept.*

ACTS 9:37, 39 | *She became ill and died. . . . The room was filled with widows who were weeping.*

You grieve over the death of a loved one.

2 CORINTHIANS 7:10 | *The kind of sorrow God wants us to experience leads us away from sin and results in salvation. There's no regret for that kind of sorrow.*

JAMES 4:9 | *Let there be tears for what you have done. Let there be sorrow and deep grief.*

You grieve over sin. It is right to genuinely grieve for your sins and beg God to remove them. Until Jesus has cleansed you of those sins, you suffer from them as they lurk within you. Confession and forgiveness will cleanse sin and wipe away the tears caused by guilt.

LUKE 13:34 | *[Jesus said,] "O Jerusalem, Jerusalem . . . ! How often I have wanted to gather your children together as a hen protects her chicks beneath her wings, but you wouldn't let me."*

When your heart is in tune with God's, you grieve for those who don't know him.

How do I get over my grief?

GENESIS 50:1 | *Joseph threw himself on his father and wept over him.*

2 SAMUEL 18:33 | *The king was overcome with emotion. He went up to the room over the gateway and burst into tears. And as he went, he cried, "O my son Absalom! My son, my son Absalom!"*

Recognize that grieving is necessary and important. You need the freedom to grieve. It is an important part of healing because it allows you to release the emotional pressure of your sorrow.

GENESIS 23:1-4 | *When Sarah was 127 years old, she died. . . . Abraham mourned and wept for her. Then, leaving her body, he said to the Hittite elders, ". . . Please sell me a piece of land so I can give my wife a proper burial."*

Take time to personally mourn, but also become involved in the steps necessary to bring closure to your loss. You grieve because you have lost something that was important to you. Being involved in the process of grieving is a way of honoring what was meaningful.

ECCLESIASTES 3:1, 4 | *For everything there is a season. . . . A time to cry and a time to laugh. A time to grieve and a time to dance.*

Grief has its season, and its season may last a long while. But eventually God wants you to move on and comfort others who grieve. When that time comes, you need to let go of your grief or risk being stuck there and unable to properly function.

ISAIAH 66:12-13 | *The LORD says: . . . "I will comfort you . . . as a mother comforts her child."*

2 CORINTHIANS 1:3 | *God is our merciful Father and the source of all comfort.*

God knows you grieve, understands your sorrow, and comforts you. He does not promise to protect you from grief, but he does promise to help you through it.

REVELATION 21:4 | *He will wipe every tear from their eyes, and there will be no more death or sorrow or crying or pain. All these things are gone forever.*

Take hope that there will be no more grieving in heaven.

How can I help others who are grieving?

PSALM 69:20 | *If only one person would show some pity; if only one would turn and comfort me.*

ROMANS 12:15 | *Weep with those who weep.*

Give your attention, sympathy, and comfort to the grieving. Pretending that the pain is not there is like rubbing salt in a wound. It is difficult to be with someone who is grieving, but you don't need to come up with the right words to make it all go away. You can't. Your concern and presence will help a grieving person more than words.

2 CORINTHIANS 1:4 | *He comforts us in all our troubles so that we can comfort others. When they are troubled, we will be able to give them the same comfort God has given us.*

Share your experiences of God's comfort. Others may begin the healing process because of you.

JOB 16:2 | *I have heard all this before. What miserable comforters you are!*

JOB 21:34 | *How can your empty clichés comfort me?*

Be careful with the words you use to those who are grieving. Explanations and clichés are rarely comforting. Love, sympathy, and the power of your presence are urgently needed. Sometimes the best comfort you can give is to just be there.

JOB 42:11 | *All his brothers, sisters, and former friends came and feasted with him in his home. And they consoled him and comforted him because of all the trials. . . . And each of them brought him a gift.*

MARK 16:10 | *[Mary] went to the disciples, who were grieving and weeping, and told them what had happened.*

You can support one another as family and friends. The Christian family must be a safe haven from a wounding world.

Promise from God PSALM 147:3 | *[The LORD] heals the brokenhearted and bandages their wounds.*

GUIDANCE

How can I experience God's guidance?

NUMBERS 9:17 | *Whenever the cloud lifted from over the sacred tent, the people of Israel would break camp and follow it.*

PROVERBS 3:5-6 | *Trust in the LORD with all your heart; do not depend on your own understanding. Seek his will in all you do, and he will show you which path to take.*

The first step in being guided is knowing where to put your trust. Travelers rely on an accurate map when they don't know where they are going. A critically ill person relies on the medical expert who knows the proper treatment. In the same way, you must realize your own spiritual limitations and rely on God's Word, which is life's instruction manual in matters of faith.

MATTHEW 7:7, 9-11 | *Keep on asking, and you will receive what you ask for. Keep on seeking, and you will find. Keep on knocking, and the door will be opened to you. . . . You parents— if your children ask for a loaf of bread, do you give them a stone*

instead? Or if they ask for a fish, do you give them a snake? Of
course not! So if you sinful people know how to give good gifts to
your children, how much more will your heavenly Father give
good gifts to those who ask him.

God invites you to pray—to go directly to him—so that
you will know him more fully as your loving Father and
understand yourself more clearly as well. Even as a parent
gives more and more responsibility to a child as he or she
grows, so the Lord expects you to take responsibility for
seeking and following his direction.

If God's will is going to happen anyway, why do I need guidance?

EXODUS 14:15 | *The LORD said to Moses, "Why are you crying*
out to me? Tell the people to get moving!"

PSALM 73:24 | *You guide me with your counsel, leading me to a*
glorious destiny.

Your choices make a difference; they impact whether you will
be participating in God's will or not. God's work will get done,
if not by you then by someone else. If you want to participate,
you can't sit around waiting for him to write a message on the
wall. Seek his guidance, and then make a decision to move
ahead. If your choices always involve asking God for guidance,
they will more often than not be in line with his will.

Will God tell me what he wants me to do for the rest of my life?

PSALM 32:8 | *The LORD says, "I will guide you along the best*
pathway for your life. I will advise you and watch over you."

PSALM 119:105 | *Your word is a lamp to guide my feet and a light for my path.*

PSALM 138:8 | *The LORD will work out his plans for my life— for your faithful love, O LORD, endures forever.*

If we could see our future, we'd either be very scared of the hard times ahead or get very cocky about our accomplishments. Instead of a searchlight that brightens a huge area, God's guidance is more like a flashlight that illuminates just enough of the path ahead to show you where to take the next few steps. God usually doesn't reveal it all at once. He wants you to learn to trust him each step of the way.

Promise from God PSALM 32:8 | *The LORD says, "I will guide you along the best pathway for your life. I will advise you and watch over you."*

HABITS

What are some of the bad habits the Bible talks about?

1 JOHN 3:8 | *When people keep on sinning, it shows that they belong to the devil, who has been sinning since the beginning.*

Sinning is a habit you cannot completely stop, but a pattern of sinful living with no change in behavior shows that you are not serious about following God.

NUMBERS 11:1 | *The people began to complain about their hardship.*

The Israelites developed a bad habit of complaining. Chronic complaining can quickly turn into bitterness.

1 TIMOTHY 5:13 | *If they are on the list [for support], [the younger widows] will learn to be lazy and will spend their time gossiping from house to house, meddling in other people's business and talking about things they shouldn't.*

Having too much time and too little to do can be fertile ground for bad habits. Idleness makes it easy to develop the bad habit of gossiping. Here Paul was urging some of the widows in the church, who had more time on their hands because the church supported them, not to fall into the habit of gossiping.

MATTHEW 15:8-9 | *These people honor me with their lips, but their hearts are far from me. Their worship is a farce, for they teach man-made ideas as commands from God.*

Engaging in religious rituals without a sincere faith is a bad habit. Make sure you haven't created habits of "worship" that God doesn't consider to be worship at all.

How can God help me deal with bad habits?

ROMANS 7:15, 25 | *[Paul said,] "I don't really understand myself, for I want to do what is right, but I don't do it. Instead, I do what I hate. . . . The answer is in Jesus Christ."*

Paul knew that he could not kick the habit of sin completely. But he also knew that, with God's help, he could make progress. In the same way, you may have to give up a habit in phases, one step at a time.

ROMANS 6:12-14 | *Do not let sin control the way you live; do not give in to sinful desires. Do not let any part of your body become an instrument . . . to serve sin. Instead, give yourselves completely to God. . . . Use your whole body as an instrument to do what is right for the glory of God. Sin is no longer your master. . . . [Now] you live under the freedom of God's grace.*

One of Satan's great lies is that you are a victim, with no power to resist some of the powerful influences around you. The world teaches you that heredity, environment, and circumstances excuse you from responsibility. But God is more powerful than anything that seeks to control you. Giving yourself completely to him allows him to use his power in your life.

1 JOHN 2:15 | *Do not love this world nor the things it offers you, for when you love the world, you do not have the love of the Father in you.*

Indulging in bad habits often feels good even though you know they are ultimately bad for you. Breaking a bad habit can be hard because you are losing something you enjoy. Understand that there may be a grieving process, but losing a bad habit ultimately brings a deeper satisfaction from doing what is pleasing to God.

COLOSSIANS 3:2 | *Think about the things of heaven, not the things of earth.*

It will be much easier to break bad habits if you replace them with good habits, which you can learn from studying Jesus' life.

What are some good habits God can help me cultivate?

HEBREWS 10:25 | *Let us not neglect our meeting together, as some people do, but encourage one another.*

Meeting with other believers is a good habit because it provides necessary support and fellowship, it enriches you as you search God's Word together, it keeps you busy when you might otherwise be slipping into bad habits, and it offers accountability.

GENESIS 26:21-22 | *Isaac's men then dug another well, but again there was a dispute over it. . . . Abandoning that one, Isaac moved on and dug another well. This time there was no dispute over it.*

Isaac pursued a habit of living in peace. In this case, it meant staying away from the source of the conflict, the Philistines, even at great personal cost.

PSALM 28:7 | *The LORD is my strength and shield. I trust him with all my heart. He helps me, and my heart is filled with joy. I burst out in songs of thanksgiving.*

As a young boy, David developed the habits of talking to God, singing songs about him, and writing psalms. These helped him to trust in and follow God all his life.

1 CORINTHIANS 9:25 | *All athletes are disciplined in their training. They do it to win a prize that will fade away, but we do it for an eternal prize.*

Good habits—such as reading God's Word, praying, and giving your time and money in service—give you spiritual stamina, purpose, and direction. They also help you keep your eyes on the ultimate goal of eternal life.

Promise from God ROMANS 8:6 | *Letting your sinful nature control your mind leads to death. But letting the Spirit control your mind leads to life and peace.*

HEALING

⎯⎯⎯⎯⎯⎯⎯⎯⎯⎯⎯⎯⎯⎯⎯⎯⎯⎯⎯⎯⎯●

From what do I need to be healed?

MARK 1:40 | *A man with leprosy came and knelt in front of Jesus, begging to be healed.*

LUKE 8:42 | *[Jairus's] only daughter, who was about twelve years old, was dying.*

Perhaps you long to be healed from sickness and disease.

ISAIAH 61:1 | *He has sent me to comfort the brokenhearted.*

Maybe you need healing and restoration from a broken heart.

PSALM 55:20 | *As for my companion, he betrayed his friends.*

You may need healing from the pain of betrayal.

PROVERBS 17:22 | *A cheerful heart is good medicine, but a broken spirit saps a person's strength.*

At times, you need healing from depression or sadness.

PSALM 103:3 | *He forgives all my sins.*

ROMANS 6:23 | *The wages of sin is death, but the free gift of God is eternal life.*

You need to be healed from sin.

How does God heal?

2 KINGS 20:7 | *Isaiah said, "Make an ointment from figs." So Hezekiah's servants spread the ointment over the boil, and Hezekiah recovered!*

Through physicians and medicine.

LUKE 5:12-13 | *"Lord," he said, "if you are willing, you can heal me and make me clean." Jesus reached out and touched him. "I am willing," he said. "Be healed!"*

Through miracles.

MARK 2:4-5 | *They couldn't bring him to Jesus because of the crowd, so they dug a hole through the roof above his head. . . . Seeing their faith, Jesus said to the paralyzed man, "My child, your sins are forgiven."*

Through the faith of friends.

PSALM 6:2 | *Heal me, LORD, for my bones are in agony.*

JAMES 5:14 | *Are any of you sick? You should call for the elders of the church to come and pray over you.*

Through prayer.

ISAIAH 38:16 | *Lord, your discipline is good, for it leads to life and health.*

Through discipline.

GENESIS 27:41; 33:4 | *Esau hated Jacob. . . . Then Esau ran to meet him and embraced him, threw his arms around his neck, and kissed him. And they both wept.*

Through time.

REVELATION 21:4 | *[God] will wipe every tear from their eyes, and there will be no more death or sorrow or crying or pain. All these things are gone forever.*

Through God's promise of heaven, for there you will receive complete and final healing.

Why doesn't God always heal people?

2 CORINTHIANS 12:9 | *My power works best in weakness.*

We do not know why God heals some and not others. But we do know that God's power is magnified through our weaknesses and infirmities if we allow him to work within us. If you have been praying for yourself or a loved one to be healed, yet God has not done what you asked, trust that he has something even greater that he wants to accomplish through the illness.

REVELATION 22:1-2 | *The angel showed me a river with the water of life, clear as crystal, flowing from the throne of God and of the Lamb. . . . On each side of the river grew a tree of life . . . [whose] leaves were used for medicine to heal the nations.*

God has full authority over all sickness. He can heal whomever he chooses. But why he heals some and not others is not known. Sometimes it is his will to release people from their suffering and sickness through death. Eventually, he will remove all sickness and suffering from all his children for eternity. You will live in heaven forever, where there will be no sickness or disease.

Promise from God MALACHI 4:2 | *For you who fear my name, the Sun of Righteousness will rise with healing in his wings. And you will go free, leaping with joy like calves let out to pasture.*

HELP

In what ways does God help me?

2 CHRONICLES 15:4 | *Whenever they were in trouble and turned to the LORD, the God of Israel, and sought him out, they found him.*

God helps you by always being available—he is present to help you whenever you call out to him. Prayer is the lifeline that connects you to God for daily help.

PHILIPPIANS 4:19 | *God . . . will supply all your needs from his glorious riches, which have been given to us in Christ Jesus.*

JAMES 1:5 | *If you need wisdom, ask our generous God, and he will give it to you. He will not rebuke you for asking.*

God helps you by providing resources to meet your needs. God has a full supply house and a ready supply system. It's free for the taking, but you must ask.

PSALM 28:7 | *The LORD is my strength and shield. I trust him with all my heart. He helps me, and my heart is filled with joy.*

God helps you by giving you strength to face any crisis. He protects you from being defeated by the enemy and gives you spiritual victory.

ISAIAH 30:21 | *Right behind you a voice will say, "This is the way you should go," whether to the right or to the left.*

God helps you through his Holy Spirit, giving you an extra measure of wisdom, discernment, and guidance.

ROMANS 8:26 | *The Holy Spirit helps us in our weakness. For example, we don't know what God wants us to pray for. But the Holy Spirit prays for us with groanings that cannot be expressed in words.*

God, through his Holy Spirit, helps you to pray, even when you don't know how to pray or what to say.

GENESIS 2:18 | *The LORD God said, "It is not good for the man to be alone. I will make a helper who is just right for him."*

God helps you by sending you other people to love and support you.

How can I help others?

1 JOHN 3:17 | *If someone has enough money to live well and sees a brother or sister in need but shows no compassion—how can God's love be in that person?*

You can help others by sharing your abundance with those who have less. Be open to the prompting of the Holy Spirit and opportunities that come to you, for they may be God asking you to be his helper.

ISAIAH 1:17 | *Learn to do good. Seek justice. Help the oppressed. Defend the cause of orphans. Fight for the rights of widows.*

God works through willing people to provide his divine help. The poor, orphans, and widows are some of many who may need your help.

ACTS 16:9 | *That night Paul had a vision: A man from Macedonia in northern Greece was standing there, pleading with him, "Come over to Macedonia and help us!"*

Tell others the good news of Jesus, giving them an opportunity to experience salvation and eternal life.

ACTS 20:28 | *Guard yourselves and God's people. Feed and shepherd God's flock—his church, purchased with his own blood—over which the Holy Spirit has appointed you as elders.*

You can help other believers grow spiritually.

GALATIANS 6:1 | *If another believer is overcome by some sin, you who are godly should gently and humbly help that person back onto the right path.*

You can help other believers who have stumbled in their walk with God, showing them how to restore their relationship with him.

Promise from God HEBREWS 13:6 | *We can say with confidence, "The LORD is my helper."*

HONESTY

Why is it so important to be honest?

PSALM 24:3-4 | *Who may climb the mountain of the LORD? Who may stand in his holy place? Only those whose hands and hearts are pure, who . . . never tell lies.*

Walking with God requires honesty, because honesty shows purity, integrity, and a desire to do what is true and right.

MATTHEW 12:33 | *A tree is identified by its fruit. If a tree is good, its fruit will be good.*

LUKE 16:10 | *If you are dishonest in little things, you won't be honest with greater responsibilities.*

Your level of honesty demonstrates the quality of your character.

1 TIMOTHY 1:19 | *Cling to your faith in Christ, and keep your conscience clear. For some people have deliberately violated their consciences; as a result, their faith has been shipwrecked.*

Honesty brings a clear conscience.

DEUTERONOMY 25:13-15 | *You must use accurate scales when you weigh out merchandise, and you must use full and honest measures . . . so that you may enjoy a long life.*

Dishonesty and deception are forms of bondage because they are needed to hide selfish motives. Honesty brings freedom from guilt and from the consequences of deceptive actions.

ROMANS 12:3 | *Be honest in your evaluation of yourselves.*

Honestly evaluating your walk with the Lord is the only way to keep growing in faith.

2 KINGS 22:7 | *Don't require the construction supervisors to keep account of the money they receive, for they are honest and trustworthy men.*

Striving for honesty helps you develop a reputation of integrity. Consistent honesty in the past and present builds trust for continued honesty in the future.

ISAIAH 33:15-16 | *Those who are honest and fair, who refuse to profit by fraud, who stay far away from bribes, . . . who shut their eyes to all enticement to do wrong—these are the ones who will dwell on high.*

Striving for honesty will help you experience the benefits of God's ultimate justice and protection.

PSALM 37:37 | *Look at those who are honest and good, for a wonderful future awaits those who love peace.*

Striving for honesty helps you to enjoy life because you can live at peace with God and yourself.

Does honesty always mean telling everything I know?

PROVERBS 29:20 | *There is more hope for a fool than for someone who speaks without thinking.*

ECCLESIASTES 3:1, 7 | *For everything there is a season, a time for every activity under heaven. . . . A time to be quiet and a time to speak.*

COLOSSIANS 4:6 | *Let your conversation be gracious and attractive so that you will have the right response for everyone.*

Honesty should not be confused with gossip. Just because you know something doesn't mean you have to tell everyone about it. Honesty also involves integrity, making sure that what you say is helpful and builds others up rather than tears them down. The person who thinks before speaking is the wisest. It is not deceitful to withhold information that others don't need to know unless, of course, you are under oath in a court of law.

Promise from God PROVERBS 12:19 | *Truthful words stand the test of time, but lies are soon exposed.*

HOPE

What can I do when my situation seems hopeless?

1 SAMUEL 1:10 | *Hannah was in deep anguish, crying bitterly as she prayed to the LORD.*

You can pray. In the midst of Hannah's hopelessness, she prayed to God, knowing that if any hope were to be found, it would be found in him.

ACTS 16:24-25 | *The jailer put them into the inner dungeon and clamped their feet in the stocks. Around midnight Paul and*

Silas were praying and singing hymns to God, and the other prisoners were listening.

You can worship. Paul and Silas were on death row for preaching about Jesus, yet in this hopeless situation they sang praises to God. Why? Because of their hope in God's promise to always be with them.

PROVERBS 10:28 | *The hopes of the godly result in happiness, but the expectations of the wicked come to nothing.*

You can focus on eternity. No matter how hopeless things seem here on earth, in Jesus you have ultimate, eternal hope. Because you know him, you have been promised a joyful eternal future in heaven. There is so much more living to do beyond the grave.

HAGGAI 1:9 | *You hoped for rich harvests, but they were poor. And when you brought your harvest home, I blew it away. Why? Because my house lies in ruins, says the LORD of Heaven's Armies, while all of you are busy building your own fine houses.*

You can persevere in putting God first, because when you follow where he leads, you know you will be going in the right direction.

How do I put my hope in God?

ROMANS 8:24 | *We were given this hope when we were saved. (If we already have something, we don't need to hope for it.)*

Hope, by definition, is expecting something that has not yet occurred. Once hope is fulfilled, it isn't hope anymore.

Thus, an important part of hope is waiting patiently for God to work.

HEBREWS 11:1 | *Faith is the confidence that what we hope for will actually happen; it gives us assurance about things we cannot see.*

Have faith in God to do what he has promised, and trust that he will. Your hopes are not idle hopes but are built on the solid foundation of his trustworthiness.

JEREMIAH 29:11 | *"I know the plans I have for you," says the LORD. "They are plans for good and not for disaster, to give you a future and a hope."*

PHILIPPIANS 3:13-14 | *Forgetting the past and looking forward to what lies ahead, I press on to reach the end of the race and receive the heavenly prize for which God, through Christ Jesus, is calling us.*

Hope involves an understanding of the future. And even here on earth God's plans are to bless, not hurt you. So if you follow his plans for you, you can look forward to your future with joyful anticipation.

How does hope help me live better today?

1 JOHN 3:3 | *All who have this eager expectation will keep themselves pure, just as [God] is pure.*

Hope is the motivating factor to help you resist temptation and keep your life pure before God.

Promise from God JOB 11:18 | *Having hope will give you courage. You will be protected and will rest in safety.*

HUMILITY

What is true humility?

ZEPHANIAH 3:12 | *Those who are left will be the lowly and humble, for it is they who trust in the name of the LORD.*

Humility is not thinking too highly of yourself.

MATTHEW 18:4 | *Anyone who becomes as humble as this little child is the greatest in the Kingdom of Heaven.*

Humility is childlike. It is an attitude of total trust in a great God.

PSALM 51:3-4 | *I recognize my rebellion; it haunts me day and night. Against you, and you alone, have I sinned; I have done what is evil in your sight. You will be proved right in what you say, and your judgment against me is just.*

Humility is willingness to admit and confess sin.

PROVERBS 12:23 | *The wise don't make a show of their knowledge, but fools broadcast their foolishness.*

Humility is refraining from proving what you know, how good you are at something, or that you are always right.

PROVERBS 13:10 | *Pride leads to conflict; those who take advice are wise.*

Humility allows you to ask for advice.

GENESIS 32:9-10 | *Jacob prayed, "O God . . . you promised me, 'I will treat you kindly.' I am not worthy of all the unfailing love and faithfulness you have shown to me, your servant."*

Humility comes when you recognize your need for God and then acknowledge how he provides for you.

How was Jesus humble?

LUKE 2:6-7 | *The time came for [Mary's] baby to be born. She gave birth to her first child, a son. She wrapped him snugly in strips of cloth and laid him in a manger, because there was no lodging available for them.*

God wanted Jesus to have a humble birth as a sign that his offer of salvation is for everyone, regardless of race or class or socioeconomic position.

ZECHARIAH 9:9 | *Rejoice, O people of Zion! Shout in triumph, O people of Jerusalem! Look, your king is coming to you. He is righteous and victorious, yet he is humble, riding on a donkey—riding on a donkey's colt.*

Jesus was King of kings, yet on his royal ride into Jerusalem, when the crowds proclaimed him king (see Matthew 21:1-11), he sat on a lowly donkey.

HEBREWS 2:9 | *Jesus . . . was given a position "a little lower than the angels"; and because he suffered death for us, he is now "crowned with glory and honor." Yes, by God's grace, Jesus tasted death for everyone.*

Jesus had all the glory and honor of sitting at God's right hand, but for your sake he gave that up to die a criminal's death so that you could be saved from eternal punishment and enjoy eternal life with him.

How do I become humble?

DEUTERONOMY 8:2-3 | *[Moses said to the people of Israel,] "Remember how the LORD your God led you through the wilderness for these forty years, humbling you and testing you to prove your character, and to find out whether or not you would obey his commands. Yes, he humbled you by letting you go hungry and then feeding you with manna. . . . He did it to teach you that people do not live by bread alone."*

Humility comes when you recognize that you need God.

1 PETER 3:8 | *All of you should be of one mind. Sympathize with each other. Love each other as brothers and sisters. Be tenderhearted, and keep a humble attitude.*

Humility comes from developing a sympathetic and tender heart toward others.

PHILIPPIANS 2:3 | *Don't be selfish; don't try to impress others. Be humble, thinking of others as better than yourselves.*

Humility means thinking of others' welfare before thinking about your own.

1 PETER 5:5 | *You younger men must accept the authority of the elders. And all of you, serve each other in humility, for "God opposes the proud but favors the humble."*

Serving other people will develop humility in you. Humility also means accepting the authority of those over you.

How does humility help me serve God better?

PHILIPPIANS 2:5-8 | *You must have the same attitude that Christ Jesus had. Though he was God, he did not think of equality with God as something to cling to. Instead, he gave up his divine privileges; he took the humble position of a slave and was born as a human being. When he appeared in human form, he humbled himself in obedience to God and died a criminal's death on a cross.*

You are humbled when you realize that God healed your soul and recognize your complete dependence on him. When you do, you're happy to serve your Lord in any way he asks.

How can humility help me deal with sin?

JAMES 4:6-10 | *[God] gives us even more grace to stand against such evil desires. As the Scriptures say, "God opposes the proud but favors the humble." So humble yourselves before God. Resist the devil, and he will flee from you. Come close to God, and God will come close to you. Wash your hands, you sinners; purify your hearts, for your loyalty is divided between God and the world. Let there be tears for what you have done. . . . Humble yourselves before the Lord, and he will lift you up in honor.*

Humility is essential to recognizing the sin in your life. Pride gives the devil the key to your heart; humility changes the lock and gives God the key. In place of pride is the humility that comes from godly sorrow for sin. Openly admit that you need God, and seek his forgiveness. No proud person can do this.

Promise from God ISAIAH 57:15 | *The high and lofty one who lives in eternity, the Holy One, says this: "I live in the high and holy place with those whose spirits are contrite and humble. I restore the crushed spirit of the humble and revive the courage of those with repentant hearts."*

INTIMACY

What must I do to experience an intimate relationship with God?

GENESIS 5:23-24 | *Enoch lived 365 years, walking in close fellowship with God. Then one day he disappeared, because God took him.*

Walk with God—daily and consistently.

EPHESIANS 5:8-10, 15 | *Once you were full of darkness, but now you have light from the Lord. So live as people of light! For this light within you produces only what is good and right and true. Carefully determine what pleases the Lord. . . . Be careful how you live. Don't live like fools, but like those who are wise.*

Live the way God wants you to live—daily and consistently.

PSALM 27:8 | *My heart has heard you say, "Come and talk with me." And my heart responds, "LORD, I am coming."*

PSALM 145:18 | *The LORD is close to all who call on him . . . in truth.*

Talk with God—daily and consistently.

JAMES 4:8 | *Come close to God, and God will come close to you. Wash your hands, you sinners; purify your hearts, for your loyalty is divided between God and the world.*

Stay close to God and always try to keep your heart pure— daily and consistently.

EXODUS 34:14 | *You must worship no other gods, for the LORD . . . is jealous about his relationship with you.*

Worship God only—daily and consistently.

MATTHEW 22:37 | *Jesus [said], "You must love the LORD your God with all your heart, all your soul, and all your mind."*

Love God completely—daily and consistently.

ROMANS 5:11 | *We can rejoice in our wonderful new relationship with God because our Lord Jesus Christ has made us friends of God.*

In light of what Jesus has done for you, put your trust in him—daily and consistently.

PSALM 1:2 | *[The godly] delight in the law of the LORD, meditating on it day and night.*

Spend time with God—daily and consistently.

What is the basis for true and lasting intimacy in marriage?

PROVERBS 5:15, 19 | *Drink water from your own well—share your love only with your wife. . . . May you always be captivated by her love.*

PROVERBS 31:10-11 | *Who can find a virtuous and capable wife? She is more precious than rubies. Her husband can trust her, and she will greatly enrich his life.*

EPHESIANS 5:24-25 | *As the church submits to Christ, so you wives should submit to your husbands. . . . For husbands, this means love your wives, just as Christ loved the church. He gave up his life for her.*

True and lasting intimacy in marriage is based upon the following: (1) being faithful to each other; (2) rejoicing in each other; (3) satisfying each other in love and sexuality; (4) accepting one's mate as a blessing from the Lord; (5) recognizing the great value of one's mate; (6) recognizing how much one's mate can truly bring delight and satisfaction; (7) living happily with each other; (8) talking together about the Lord and spiritual things; (9) giving thanks to the Lord together; (10) submitting to each other; and (11) loving each other as passionately as Christ loved the church and died for it.

Promise from God   1 CHRONICLES 28:9 | *Learn to know the God of your ancestors intimately. Worship and serve him with your whole heart and a willing mind. For the LORD sees every heart and knows every plan and thought. If you seek him, you will find him.*

JEALOUSY

Why is jealousy so dangerous?

PROVERBS 14:30 | *A peaceful heart leads to a healthy body; jealousy is like cancer in the bones.*

Jealousy eats away at you because it causes you to feed on the destructive emotions of anger and bitterness rather than be content with what you have and genuinely happy for the success of others.

GENESIS 37:11, 18, 24, 28 | *[Joseph's] brothers were jealous of Joseph. . . . When Joseph's brothers saw him coming, . . . they grabbed him and threw him into the cistern. . . . So when the*

Ishmaelites, who were Midianite traders, came by, Joseph's brothers pulled him out of the cistern and sold him to them for twenty pieces of silver. And the traders took him to Egypt.

PROVERBS 27:4 | *Anger is cruel . . . but jealousy is even more dangerous.*

Jealousy is divisive and often tears families and friends apart because it embraces a spirit of negative competition.

1 SAMUEL 18:9-11 | *Saul kept a jealous eye on David. . . . David was playing the harp, as he did each day. But Saul had a spear in his hand, and he suddenly hurled it at David, intending to pin him to the wall.*

ACTS 17:5-6 | *Some of the Jews were jealous, so they gathered some troublemakers from the marketplace to form a mob and start a riot. They attacked the home of Jason, searching for Paul and Silas so they could drag them out to the crowd. Not finding them there, they dragged out Jason and some of the other believers instead.*

Jealousy for attention or affection can drive people to extreme action, even seeking to harm or kill others. Envy and jealousy not only destroy the people who feel them but often lead these people to attack the objects of their envy and jealousy. While you may not attack a person with a spear as Saul did, you may use sharp words and piercing comments, which can be potentially as dangerous.

How can I deal with jealousy?

GENESIS 30:1 | *When Rachel saw that she wasn't having any children for Jacob, she became jealous of her sister.*

Instead of enjoying the favor and love of her husband, Rachel focused on her inability to give Jacob children. She became jealous of her sister, Leah. The cure for jealousy is being thankful and enjoying what you have instead of focusing on what you don't have.

MATTHEW 20:15 | *Should you be jealous because I am kind to others?*

Jealousy reveals selfishness. You want for yourself what someone else has. Rejoicing in another's success or good fortune will increase your own capacity for joy.

JOHN 21:19-22 | *Jesus said this to let [Peter] know by what kind of death he would glorify God. . . . Peter turned around and saw behind them the disciple Jesus loved. . . . Peter asked Jesus, "What about him, Lord?" Jesus replied, "If I want him to remain alive until I return, what is that to you? As for you, follow me."*

When Peter heard Jesus' prophecy of his death, he wondered what would happen to the other disciple (John). Jesus made it clear that Peter was to pay attention to his own concerns, not those of others. In many situations you may be tempted to compare your lot in life with another's. Instead, keep your focus on what you believe God wants you to do, and accept that his will for you is best.

Promise from God PROVERBS 14:30 | *A peaceful heart leads to a healthy body; jealousy is like cancer in the bones.*

JOY

How can I find real and lasting joy?

PSALM 86:4 | *Give me happiness, O Lord, for I give myself to you.*

PSALM 146:5 | *Joyful are those who have the God of Israel as their helper, whose hope is in the LORD their God.*

The Lord himself is the source of true joy. The more you love him, know him, walk with him, and become like him, the greater your joy will be.

PSALM 112:1 | *How joyful are those who fear the LORD and delight in obeying his commands.*

It seems ironic that the more you fear the Lord, the more joyful you will be. But the Bible says that to fear the Lord (to respect him so much you want to listen to what he says) is the way to wisdom. Wisdom helps you make good choices that bring joy and helps you avoid harmful choices that bring misery.

MATTHEW 25:21 | *You have been faithful in handling this small amount. . . . Let's celebrate together!*

A job well done brings a deep sense of satisfaction and is an occasion for joy.

How can I be joyful when faced with difficult circumstances?

2 CORINTHIANS 12:9-10 | *Each time [God] said, "My grace is all you need. My power works best in weakness." So now I am glad*

. . . about my weaknesses, so that the power of Christ can work through me. . . . For when I am weak, then I am strong.

1 PETER 4:12-13 | *Don't be surprised at the fiery trials you are going through, as if something strange were happening to you. Instead, be very glad—for . . . you will have the wonderful joy of seeing [Christ's] glory.*

God promises a reward when you endure difficult circumstances because of your faith. Anticipating this eternal reward gives you joy in the middle of adversity. Temporary suffering will be replaced by a greater joy that lasts.

HEBREWS 10:34 | *You suffered along with those who were thrown into jail, and when all you owned was taken from you, you accepted it with joy. You knew there were better things waiting for you that will last forever.*

Hope in God's promises of eternal life can give you joy because you know that what you are presently going through will one day end.

How can I bring God joy?

DEUTERONOMY 30:10 | *The LORD your God will delight in you if you obey his voice and keep the commands and decrees written in this Book of Instruction, and if you turn to the LORD your God with all your heart and soul.*

PROVERBS 15:8 | *The LORD . . . delights in the prayers of the upright.*

PROVERBS 15:26 | *The LORD . . . delights in pure words.*

Can finite, sinful human beings truly bring joy and delight to the Lord, the Creator of the universe? He says yes. God created you because he wants to have a relationship with you, to delight in being with you. But you must also want a relationship with him. A good relationship goes both ways and is built on principles that are simple to understand but difficult to practice: trust, regular communication, humility to admit your mistakes, devoted service, and unconditional love.

Promise from God PSALM 119:35 | *Make me walk along the path of your commands, for that is where my happiness is found.*

JUSTICE

Is God always fair and just?

2 THESSALONIANS 1:5-6 | *God will use . . . persecution to show his justice and . . . in his justice he will pay back those who persecute you.*

When you are burdened with trouble, it is tempting to think God is not fair or just. How can he allow a Christian to suffer, when so many dishonest people are prospering? But God has made it clear in the Bible that justice and fairness, while always right, will often be perverted in this life by selfish people. The Bible also makes it clear that justice will not be twisted forever. True justice will one day prevail, forever, for those who follow God.

EZRA 9:15 | *O LORD, God of Israel, you are just. We come before you in our guilt . . . in such a condition none of us can stand in your presence.*

Don't beg God for justice, because he might have to punish you. Instead, beg for his love so he will forgive you. Don't beg God for fairness, because that might bring judgment. Instead, beg for mercy so you can be saved. Part of God's justice is granting mercy to those with sincere hearts.

How can I work effectively for justice?

AMOS 5:21, 24 | *[The Lord says,] "I hate all your show and pretense—the hypocrisy of your religious festivals and solemn assemblies. . . . Instead, I want to see a mighty flood of justice, an endless river of righteous living."*

Make justice a top priority.

PSALM 82:3 | *Give justice to the poor and the orphan; uphold the rights of the oppressed and the destitute.*

Speak out against injustice.

PSALM 59:1-2 | *Rescue me from my enemies, O God. Protect me from those who have come to destroy me. Rescue me from these criminals; save me from these murderers.*

Pray that God will intervene where injustice prevails.

ISAIAH 1:17 | *Learn to do good. Seek justice. Help the oppressed. Defend the cause of orphans. Fight for the rights of widows.*

Strive for justice with energy and dedication.

PSALM 106:3 | *There is joy for those who deal justly with others and always do what is right.*

ISAIAH 56:1 | *The LORD says: "Be just and fair to all. Do what is right and good, for I am coming soon to rescue you and to display my righteousness among you."*

ROMANS 13:7 | *Give to everyone what you owe them.*

Persist in doing what is right. Don't become unjust yourself.

How do God's justice and mercy relate?

2 SAMUEL 24:14 | *Let us fall into the hands of the LORD, for his mercy is great.*

ROMANS 6:23 | *The wages of sin is death, but the free gift of God is eternal life through Christ Jesus our Lord.*

God is just in that he very clearly tells you what sin is and what its consequences will be. Justice is getting what you deserve for your sin. God is merciful in that he offers a way for you to be spared the punishment you deserve. Grace is getting what you don't deserve—forgiveness for your sins and friendship with God.

MATTHEW 5:43-44 | *[Jesus said,] "You have heard the law that says, 'Love your neighbor' and hate your enemy. But I say, love your enemies!"*

Justice punishes evil, crime, and wrongdoing. Mercy forgives the sinner. Jesus sets a new standard for mercy. One of the hardest things you can do is forgive someone who has wronged you, but it is only through forgiveness that you can be free of the bitterness of injustice. Your mercy may be exactly what someone needs to understand God's mercy.

Promise from God PSALM 58:11 | *Then at last everyone will say, "There truly is a reward for those who live for God; surely there is a God who judges justly here on earth."*

LISTENING

Why is listening so important?

PROVERBS 1:9 | *What you learn from [your father and mother] will crown you with grace and be a chain of honor around your neck.*

Listening helps you grow and mature. Good listening fosters learning, which leads to knowledge and wisdom.

PROVERBS 5:13-14 | *Oh, why didn't I listen to my teachers? Why didn't I pay attention to my instructors? I have come to the brink of utter ruin, and now I must face public disgrace.*

Listening helps keep you from making mistakes you could have avoided.

PROVERBS 2:1, 9 | *My child, listen to what I say, and treasure my commands. . . . Then you will understand what is right . . . and you will find the right way to go.*

Listening to God is essential to making good decisions. When you truly listen to the Holy Spirit and to God's commands, you will have the guidance you need to make wise choices.

PROVERBS 8:6 | *Listen to me! For I have important things to tell you.*

Listening keeps you from being closed minded. It gives you the opportunity to hear a variety of ideas from many different sources.

EXODUS 18:24 | *Moses listened to his father-in-law's advice and followed his suggestions.*

Listening shows that you respect others. It honors their words, and they feel affirmed because you've listened to them.

What are some things I shouldn't listen to?

GENESIS 3:1, 6 | *[The serpent] asked the woman, "Did God really say you must not eat the fruit from any of the trees in the garden?" . . . She saw that the tree was beautiful and its fruit looked delicious, and she wanted the wisdom it would give her. So she took some of the fruit and ate it.*

MATTHEW 6:13 | *Don't let us yield to temptation.*

Temptation.

LEVITICUS 19:16 | *Do not spread slanderous gossip among your people.*

Gossip.

MARK 13:21-23 | *If anyone tells you, "Look, here is the Messiah," or "There he is," don't believe it. For false messiahs and false prophets will rise up and perform signs and wonders so as to deceive, if possible, even God's chosen ones. Watch out!*

False teaching.

EPHESIANS 5:4 | *Obscene stories, foolish talk, and coarse jokes— these are not for you.*

Insults and off-color stories.

PROVERBS 13:5 | *The godly hate lies.*

Lies.

PROVERBS 29:5 | *To flatter friends is to lay a trap for their feet.*

Flattery.

How can I better listen to God?

PSALM 5:3 | *Each morning I bring my requests to you and wait expectantly.*

Through prayer. After you talk to God, stay and listen for a while.

PSALM 46:10 | *Be still, and know that I am God!*

Being quiet helps you better hear God's voice. Find times and places where there's nothing else to hear but God's voice.

LUKE 8:18 | *Pay attention to how you hear. To those who listen to my teaching, more understanding will be given. But for those who are not listening, even what they think they understand will be taken away from them.*

When you think you've heard something from God, pay attention to it. Don't miss an opportunity for a lesson from the Master Teacher.

Promise from God PROVERBS 1:23 | *Come and listen to my counsel. I'll share my heart with you and make you wise.*

LONELINESS

Why does God allow me to be lonely?

GENESIS 2:18 | *The LORD God said, "It is not good for the man to be alone. I will make a helper who is just right for him."*

God did not intend for you to be lonely. On the contrary, it was God who recognized Adam's need for companionship.

He gave Adam the task of naming the animals so that Adam could recognize his need for a human companion. It was then that God created woman (see Genesis 2:19-22).

1 SAMUEL 20:41 | *David bowed three times to Jonathan. . . . Both of them were in tears as they embraced each other and said good-bye, especially David.*

1 THESSALONIANS 2:17 | *Dear brothers and sisters, after we were separated from you for a little while (though our hearts never left you), we tried very hard to come back because of our intense longing to see you again.*

You live in a sinful, fallen world. Therefore, you will often be separated from friends and family for various reasons. Sometimes you are lonely because you have hurt those you care about and they have left you. Sometimes your friends stop being your friends for reasons you don't understand. And sometimes you have to say good-bye when a friend moves away. In each of these circumstances, he promises to help you learn from it, and he promises to never leave you, always supplying you with comfort and strength when you ask (see Deuteronomy 31:8; Philippians 4:19).

ROMANS 8:38-39 | *Nothing can ever separate us from God's love. . . . Not even the powers of hell can separate us from God's love. . . . Indeed, nothing in all creation will ever be able to separate us from the love of God that is revealed in Christ Jesus our Lord.*

God has promised he will always be there for you. Nothing can separate you from him. When your human relationships fail, take comfort from your friendship with God.

How can God help me with loneliness?

PSALM 139:17 | *How precious are your thoughts about me, O God. They cannot be numbered!*

Recognize that you are not unlovable or deficient just because you are lonely. You have value because God made you, loves you, and promises never to leave you.

1 KINGS 19:4 | *[Elijah] went on alone into the wilderness, traveling all day. He sat down under a solitary broom tree and prayed that he might die.*

Loneliness can cause you to feel sorry for yourself, become discouraged, and fall prey to temptation. Don't give up on God when you are lonely. Be careful not to separate yourself from the One who wants to be with you always.

1 KINGS 19:10 | *Elijah [said], ". . . I am the only one left, and now they are trying to kill me, too."*

1 PETER 4:19 | *If you are suffering in a manner that pleases God, keep on doing what is right, and trust your lives to the God who created you, for he will never fail you.*

Sometimes you may feel alone in your stand for Christ. Take comfort in knowing that there are others who are equally committed and that God rewards your bold commitment to him.

ROMANS 12:4-5 | *Just as our bodies have many parts and each part has a special function, so it is with Christ's body. We are many parts of one body, and we all belong to each other.*

HEBREWS 10:25 | *Let us not neglect our meeting together, as some people do, but encourage one another, especially now that the day of his return is drawing near.*

The best way to avoid loneliness is to get together with other believers. Get involved in a local church. Get busy with God's people, doing God's work.

How can I help those who are lonely?

JAMES 1:27 | *Pure and genuine religion in the sight of God the Father means caring for orphans and widows in their distress.*

3 JOHN 1:5 | *You are being faithful to God when you care for the traveling teachers who pass through, even though they are strangers to you.*

Invite lonely people into your home or visit them and befriend them. Often in caring for those who are lonely, your need for company will be met as well.

Promise from God HEBREWS 13:5 | *God has said, "I will never fail you. I will never abandon you."*

LOVE

What is love?

1 CORINTHIANS 13:4-7 | *Love is patient and kind. Love is not jealous or boastful or proud or rude. It does not demand its own way. It is not irritable, and it keeps no record of being wronged. It does not rejoice about injustice but rejoices whenever the*

truth wins out. Love never gives up, never loses faith, is always hopeful, and endures through every circumstance.

These famous verses about love are some of the most eloquent and accurate descriptions of love ever written. Love is a commitment and a choice of conduct that produces powerful feelings. If you practice the qualities and behaviors described in these verses, you will experience satisfaction and fulfillment beyond imagination.

JOHN 15:13 | *There is no greater love than to lay down one's life for one's friends.*

Love is willing to sacrifice for the good of others, even unto death.

Why should I love God?

MARK 12:29-30; JOHN 14:23 | *Jesus [said], "The most important commandment is this: . . . You must love the LORD your God with all your heart, all your soul, all your mind, and all your strength. . . . All who love me will do what I say. My Father will love them, and we will come and make our home with each of them."*

JOHN 15:9-11 | *[Jesus said,] "I have loved you even as the Father has loved me. Remain in my love. When you obey my commandments, you remain in my love, just as I obey my Father's commandments and remain in his love. I have told you these things so that you will be filled with my joy. Yes, your joy will overflow!"*

When you love God, you are made holy in his eyes, you experience his very presence and power, you allow his

Spirit to live in you, you enjoy his wisdom and guidance, and you are assured of living forever with him in heaven. God does, however, require your love for him to be sincere and consuming—with all your heart, soul, mind, and strength.

PSALM 116:1 | *I love the LORD because he hears my voice and my prayer for mercy.*

Love God because he listens to you. God's listening involves an understanding of you that no one else can have.

1 JOHN 3:1 | *See how very much our Father loves us.*

Love God because he loves you and desires a relationship with you.

How should I show my love to God?

JOHN 14:21 | *Those who accept my commandments and obey them are the ones who love me.*

Love God by obeying him and respecting his commandments.

PSALM 122:1 | *I was glad when they said to me, "Let us go to the house of the LORD."*

Love God by worshiping him and praising him for his love for you.

HEBREWS 6:10 | *[God] will not forget . . . how you have shown your love to him by caring for other believers.*

Love God by helping others and being a Christlike example to them.

Promise from God ROMANS 8:39 | *No power in the sky above or in the earth below—indeed, nothing in all creation will ever be able to separate us from the love of God that is revealed in Christ Jesus our Lord.*

MARRIAGE

What are the keys to a happy, strong marriage?

JOSHUA 24:15 | *Choose today whom you will serve. . . . As for me and my family, we will serve the LORD.*

A united purpose to serve the Lord.

HEBREWS 13:4 | *Give honor to marriage, and remain faithful to one another in marriage.*

Faithfulness. Without faithfulness there is no real trust or intimacy.

ROMANS 15:1-2 | *We must not just please ourselves. We should help others do what is right and build them up in the Lord.*

Self-sacrifice. This means thinking of your spouse's needs and interests first.

ROMANS 15:5-6 | *May God . . . help you live in complete harmony with each other, as is fitting for followers of Christ Jesus. Then all of you can join together with one voice, giving praise and glory to God.*

Understanding and celebrating each other's differences.

EPHESIANS 5:21, 33 | *Submit to one another out of reverence for Christ. . . . Each man must love his wife as he loves himself, and the wife must respect her husband.*

Mutual submission.

1 CORINTHIANS 13:4-5 | *Love is patient and kind. Love is not jealous or boastful or proud or rude. It does not demand its own way. It is not irritable, and it keeps no record of being wronged.*

Unconditional love.

JAMES 5:16 | *Confess your sins to each other and pray for each other.*

Praying with and for each other.

PROVERBS 5:18-19 | *Rejoice in the wife of your youth. . . . Let her breasts satisfy you always. May you always be captivated by her love.*

SONG OF SONGS 1:2 | *Kiss me and kiss me again, for your love is sweeter than wine.*

1 CORINTHIANS 7:3 | *The husband should fulfill his wife's sexual needs, and the wife should fulfill her husband's needs.*

A healthy sex life.

How can I show my affection for my spouse?

EPHESIANS 5:25 | *Husbands . . . love your wives, just as Christ loved the church. He gave up his life for her.*

Christ loved the church enough to die for it. Commit that your love for your spouse will be as strong.

SONG OF SONGS 7:11 | *Come, my love, let us go out to the fields and spend the night among the wildflowers.*

Spending time with each other communicates your level of affection for each other. Make it a priority to find things you enjoy doing together.

SONG OF SONGS 1:9 | *You are as exciting, my darling, as a mare among Pharaoh's stallions.*

Verbally express your affection for your spouse. Don't concentrate on your spouse's faults because this will cause him or her to focus on yours. Instead, find things to appreciate, and then express them. Your spouse will usually respond likewise.

SONG OF SONGS 1:12 | *The king is lying on his couch, enchanted by the fragrance of my perfume.*

Look for ways to please each other. People experience love in different ways. Scent seems to be one way that Solomon experienced love or pleasure. Ask your spouse what pleases him or her most, and make an effort to experience that together.

What if I have already married an unbeliever? Should we stay together?

1 CORINTHIANS 7:12-14, 16 | *If a Christian man has a wife who is not a believer and she is willing to continue living with him, he must not leave her. And if a Christian woman has a husband who is not a believer and he is willing to continue living with her, she must not leave him. For the Christian wife brings holiness to her marriage, and the Christian husband brings holiness to his marriage. . . . Don't you wives realize that your husbands might be saved because of you? And don't you husbands realize that your wives might be saved because of you?*

Don't leave your spouse just because he or she isn't a Christian. If possible, win your spouse to Christ with your love. But if that doesn't happen, continue to love him or her as Christ loved, sacrificially and unselfishly. Take your situation to God and ask him to draw your spouse to him. Also, pray that your faith will grow stronger so that you will not be tempted to fall away.

Promise from God EPHESIANS 5:31 | *As the Scriptures say, "A man leaves his father and mother and is joined to his wife, and the two are united into one."*

MERCY

How does God show me mercy?

PSALM 103:3-5 | *[The LORD] forgives all my sins. . . . He redeems me from death. . . . He fills my life with good things.*

God showers numerous acts of mercy on you each day. Anything good in your life is from God's merciful hand.

EXODUS 34:6 | *The LORD! The God of compassion and mercy! I am slow to anger and filled with unfailing love and faithfulness.*

EPHESIANS 2:4-5 | *God is so rich in mercy, and he loved us so much, that even though we were dead because of our sins, he gave us life.*

God shows you mercy by being slow to get angry over your sins, by offering you eternal life and salvation, and by showing you unfailing love no matter what you have done against him.

TITUS 3:4-7 | *When God our Savior revealed his kindness and love, he saved us, not because of the righteous things we had done, but because of his mercy. He washed away our sins, giving us a new birth and new life through the Holy Spirit. He generously poured out the Spirit upon us through Jesus Christ our Savior. Because of his grace he declared us righteous and gave us confidence that we will inherit eternal life.*

By God's love you were given the free gift of salvation even though you didn't deserve it. Because of God's mercy, you have received forgiveness and freedom from guilt. Through God's kindness, you have been blessed beyond your wildest dreams because you have secured a perfect life for all eternity in heaven.

How can I show mercy?

COLOSSIANS 3:12-13 | *Since God chose you to be the holy people he loves, you must clothe yourselves with tenderhearted mercy, kindness, humility, gentleness, and patience. Make allowance for each other's faults, and forgive anyone who offends you. Remember, the Lord forgave you, so you must forgive others.*

Because God has forgiven you, you must follow his example of mercy and forgive others.

MATTHEW 18:33 | *Shouldn't you have mercy . . . just as I had mercy on you?*

Be merciful to others even when they don't deserve it.

MICAH 6:8 | *O people, the LORD has told you what is good, and this is what he requires of you: to do what is right, to love mercy, and to walk humbly with your God.*

When you obey God sincerely, your life will overflow with merciful acts.

ZECHARIAH 7:9 | *This is what the LORD of Heaven's Armies says: Judge fairly, and show mercy and kindness to one another.*

You can show mercy by judging fairly and honestly and by showing kindness to others.

Promise from God LUKE 1:50 | *He shows mercy from generation to generation to all who fear him.*

MISTAKES

What does the Bible say about mistakes?

GENESIS 3:11-13 | *[God asked,] "Have you eaten from the tree whose fruit I commanded you not to eat?" The man replied, "It was the woman you gave me who gave me the fruit, and I ate it." Then the LORD God asked the woman, "What have you done?" "The serpent deceived me," she replied. "That's why I ate it."*

Both Adam and Eve responded to mistakes by trying to shift blame to someone else rather than taking responsibility for their actions.

JUDGES 16:17, 21, 28 | *Finally, Samson shared his secret with her. . . . So the Philistines captured him and gouged out his eyes. . . . Then Samson prayed to the LORD, "Sovereign LORD, remember me again."*

Samson's life, although filled with foolish mistakes, was still mightily used by God.

JONAH 1:3 | *Jonah . . . went in the opposite direction to get away from the LORD.*

Jonah made the worst mistake: running from God.

EXODUS 2:12; 33:17 | *After looking in all directions to make sure no one was watching, Moses killed the Egyptian and hid the body in the sand. . . . The LORD [said] to Moses, "I will indeed do what you have asked, for I look favorably on you, and I know you by name."*

Even Moses' life was marred by an immature and terrible mistake, yet God forgave him and had a special relationship with him.

MATTHEW 26:74-75; 16:18-19; JOHN 21:16 | *Peter swore, "A curse on me if I'm lying—I don't know the man!" And immediately the rooster crowed. . . . And he went away, weeping bitterly. . . . [Jesus said,] "Now I say to you that you are Peter (which means 'rock'), and upon this rock I will build my church, and all the powers of hell will not conquer it. And I will give you the keys of the Kingdom of Heaven." . . . Jesus [asked]: ". . . Do you love me?" "Yes, Lord," Peter said, "you know I love you." "Then take care of my sheep," Jesus said.*

Christ restored Peter to fellowship—and leadership—even after his most painful mistake.

JAMES 3:2 | *Indeed, we all make many mistakes. For if we could control our tongues, we would be perfect and could also control ourselves in every other way.*

The Bible says that one of the most common mistakes is speaking and later regretting it.

When I make a big mistake, how do I move on?

2 SAMUEL 12:13 | *David confessed to Nathan, "I have sinned against the LORD." Nathan replied, "Yes, but the LORD has forgiven you."*

Begin by admitting your mistakes and sins so you are open to forgiveness and restoration of your relationships.

1 JOHN 1:9 | *If we confess our sins to him, he is faithful and just to forgive us.*

Receive God's forgiveness. He wants to give it as much as you need to receive it.

JAMES 5:16 | *Confess your sins to each other and pray for each other.*

Offer forgiveness to others, ask for theirs when needed, and receive it when it's extended.

JEREMIAH 8:4-6 | *This is what the LORD says: "When people fall down, don't they get up again? When they discover they're on the wrong road, don't they turn back? Then why do these people stay on their self-destructive path? Why do the people of Jerusalem refuse to turn back? . . . Is anyone sorry for doing wrong? Does anyone say, 'What a terrible thing I have done'?"*

Don't be afraid of making mistakes. If you never make mistakes, it's because you've never tried to succeed. And once you're forgiven, don't linger on your mistakes. Let them go, and walk through the doorway to your future. Learning from your past mistakes prepares you to not repeat them in the future.

Promise from God PHILIPPIANS 3:13-14 | *No, dear brothers and sisters, I have not achieved it, but I focus on this one thing: Forgetting the past and looking forward to what lies ahead, I press on to reach the end of the race and receive the heavenly prize for which God, through Christ Jesus, is calling us.*

MONEY

What is a proper perspective toward money?

MATTHEW 6:21 | *Wherever your treasure is, there the desires of your heart will also be.*

The Bible mentions many wealthy people who loved God while saying nothing negative about the amount of wealth they owned (Abraham, David, Joseph of Arimathea, Lydia). Scripture doesn't focus on how much money you can or cannot have, but rather on what you do with it. Jesus made one thing clear: Wherever your money goes, your heart will follow after it. So work hard and succeed without guilt, but make sure to work just as hard at finding ways to please God with your money.

PSALM 23:1 | *The LORD is my shepherd; I have all that I need.*

ECCLESIASTES 5:10 | *Those who love money will never have enough. How meaningless to think that wealth brings true happiness!*

Money can cultivate a dangerous craving—the more you have, the more you want. It is a vicious cycle that never has a satisfactory conclusion. Keep reminding yourself that God must be first in your life and that money cannot satisfy your deepest needs.

MATTHEW 6:24 | *No one can serve two masters. . . . You cannot serve both God and money.*

1 TIMOTHY 6:10 | *The love of money is the root of all kinds of evil. And some people, craving money, have wandered from the true faith and pierced themselves with many sorrows.*

HEBREWS 13:5 | *Don't love money; be satisfied with what you have.*

Money is not the root of all evil; the love of it is!

PROVERBS 19:1 | *Better to be poor and honest than to be dishonest and a fool.*

MARK 8:36 | *What do you benefit if you gain the whole world but lose your own soul?*

No amount of money is worth having if it was gained deceptively or dishonestly. Taking advantage of others to make money is stealing. Those who do this lose far more than they could ever gain.

1 JOHN 3:17 | *If someone has enough money to live well and sees a brother or sister in need but shows no compassion—how can God's love be in that person?*

When your giving meets needs in the lives of others, you will find much deeper satisfaction than if you had spent the money on yourself—or kept it.

MALACHI 3:10 | *"Bring all the tithes into the storehouse so there will be enough food in my Temple. If you do," says the LORD of Heaven's Armies, "I will open the windows of heaven for you.*

I will pour out a blessing so great you won't have enough room to take it in! Try it! Put me to the test!"

Instead of viewing money as yours to use as you wish, see it as God's to use as he wishes. Giving back to God the first part of everything you receive will help you maintain this perspective.

Is debt a sin?

MATTHEW 18:23 | *[Jesus said,] "The Kingdom of Heaven can be compared to a king who decided to bring his accounts up to date with servants who had borrowed money from him."*

In teaching on forgiveness, Jesus used this parable that seems to assume the lending or borrowing of money is not itself sinful.

PROVERBS 22:7 | *Just as the rich rule the poor, so the borrower is servant to the lender.*

Although borrowing money is not, in itself, sinful, you must be careful and wise when you borrow so you don't become a slave to debt.

ROMANS 13:8 | *Owe nothing to anyone—except for your obligation to love one another.*

Although incurring debt may not be sinful, the failure to repay a debt is.

Promise from God MATTHEW 6:31-33 | *Don't worry about these things, saying, "What will we eat? What will we drink? What will we wear?" . . . Your heavenly Father already knows all your needs. Seek the Kingdom of God above all else, and live righteously, and he will give you everything you need.*

MOTIVES

Do my motives matter?

1 CHRONICLES 29:17 | *I know, my God, that you examine our hearts and rejoice when you find integrity there. You know I have done all this with good motives, and I have watched your people offer their gifts willingly and joyously.*

PROVERBS 20:27 | *The LORD's light penetrates the human spirit, exposing every hidden motive.*

Your motives are very important to God—the condition of your heart is essential to the condition of your relationship with God.

MATTHEW 6:1 | *Don't do your good deeds publicly, to be admired by others, for you will lose the reward from your Father in heaven.*

When you pursue spiritual life with self-serving motives, you rob yourself of the joy God intends.

1 SAMUEL 16:7 | *The LORD said to Samuel, "Don't judge by his appearance or height. . . . The LORD doesn't see things the way you see them. People judge by outward appearance, but the LORD looks at the heart."*

God is more concerned about your motives than your appearance or outward actions because your motives determine what is in your heart.

JAMES 4:3 | *When you ask, you don't get it because your motives are all wrong—you want only what will give you pleasure.*

Wrong motives can hinder your prayers when selfishness rules your requests.

How can I have purer motives?

PSALM 19:14 | *May the words of my mouth and the meditation of my heart be pleasing to you, O LORD, my rock and my redeemer.*

Ask God to change the way you think by changing your heart.

1 CHRONICLES 28:9 | *Learn to know . . . God . . . intimately. Worship and serve him with your whole heart and a willing mind. For the LORD sees every heart and knows every plan and thought.*

Your attitude toward God is a good indicator of your motives toward others. If you are halfhearted in the way you approach your relationship with God, chances are your motives toward others may be more halfhearted and self-centered than they should be.

PSALM 26:2 | *Put me on trial, LORD, and cross-examine me. Test my motives and my heart.*

PROVERBS 17:3 | *Fire tests the purity of silver and gold, but the LORD tests the heart.*

Welcome it when God tests your motives. This gives you an opportunity to grow.

PROVERBS 21:2 | *People may be right in their own eyes, but the LORD examines their heart.*

Before you do something, remember that God is as interested in your motives as he is in your actions.

Promise from God   EZEKIEL 36:26 | *[The Lord says,] "I will give you a new heart, and I will put a new spirit in you. I will take out your stony, stubborn heart and give you a tender, responsive heart."*

OBEDIENCE

Is obedience to God really necessary, since I am saved by faith?

JOHN 14:15 | *[Jesus said,] "If you love me, obey my commandments."*

1 JOHN 3:24 | *Those who obey God's commandments remain in fellowship with him, and he with them. And we know he lives in us because the Spirit he gave us lives in us.*

God's commandments are not burdensome obligations but pathways to joyful, meaningful, satisfying lives. And obeying God is the only way to stay in fellowship with him. God's call for your obedience is based on his own commitment to your well-being. Since God is the Creator of life, he knows how life is supposed to work. Obedience demonstrates your willingness to follow through on what he says, your trust that God's way is best for you, and your desire to have a close relationship with him.

In what ways does God want me to obey him?

GENESIS 6:22 | *Noah did everything exactly as God had commanded him.*

DEUTERONOMY 5:32 | *You must be careful to obey all the commands of the LORD your God, following his instructions in every detail.*

Obedience is not about "generally" following God's commands or following any of his instructions that suit you. True obedience is about following every detail of all his commands to the best of your ability.

Does obedience to God get me into heaven?

GALATIANS 2:16 | *A person is made right with God by faith in Jesus Christ, not by obeying the law. . . . For no one will ever be made right with God by obeying the law.*

Obedience to religious laws or rules is not what saves you for eternity. But when you believe in Jesus and decide to follow him, you are increasingly motivated to obey God out of love for him.

HEBREWS 11:8 | *It was by faith that Abraham obeyed.*

Obedience is motivated by faith, but obedience itself is not the way to heaven; only faith in Jesus Christ as Savior will get you to heaven. Obedience is the result of faith, not the pathway to faith.

What if I have lived a life of disobedience?

MATTHEW 21:28-31 | *[Jesus said,] "A man with two sons told the older boy, 'Son, go out and work in the vineyard today.' The son answered, 'No, I won't go,' but later he changed his mind and went anyway. Then the father told the other son, 'You go,' and he said, 'Yes, sir, I will.' But he didn't go. Which of the two obeyed his father?"*

It's never too late to stop a life of disobedience to God and start a life of obedience to him. All it takes is to be genuinely sorry for your sins and ask God to forgive you so you can start over.

How will the Lord help me obey him?

PHILIPPIANS 2:12-13 | *Work hard to show the results of your salvation, obeying God with deep reverence and fear. For God is working in you, giving you the desire and the power to do what pleases him.*

What God requires, God empowers. Not only does God guide you into the ways that are best for you, but he also gives you the power to live according to those ways.

JOHN 14:15-17 | *[Jesus said,] "If you love me, obey my commandments. And I will ask the Father, and he will give you another Advocate, who will never leave you. He is the Holy Spirit, who leads into all truth. . . . You know him, because he lives with you now and later will be in you."*

The power God gives you is his own Holy Spirit, who is also called an Advocate. As an advocate, he comes alongside you not only to advise and inspire you but actually to live and work in you. Even as the air you breathe empowers your physical body, so the Holy Spirit empowers your obedience.

Promise from God HEBREWS 8:10 | *This is the new covenant I will make with the . . . people: I will put my laws in their minds, and I will write them on their hearts. I will be their God, and they will be my people.*

OPPORTUNITIES

How do I know if an opportunity is from God?

1 THESSALONIANS 5:17 | *Never stop praying.*

The closer you stay to God through prayer, the easier it is to hear his voice.

JOSHUA 1:7 | *Be strong and very courageous. Be careful to obey all the instructions Moses gave you. Do not deviate from them, turning either to the right or to the left. Then you will be successful in everything you do.*

PSALM 119:105 | *Your word is a lamp to guide my feet and a light for my path.*

Though the Bible will not always speak directly about a particular opportunity, any opportunity that contradicts God's Word or leads you away from its principles is not from God.

PROVERBS 15:22 | *Plans go wrong for lack of advice; many advisers bring success.*

Seek the wisdom of trustworthy, mature Christians.

MATTHEW 25:21 | *Well done, my good and faithful servant. You have been faithful in handling this small amount, so now I will give you many more responsibilities.*

God presents everyone with the ability and the opportunity to invest for the good and the growth of his Kingdom.

PHILIPPIANS 1:12 | *I want you to know, my dear brothers and sisters, that everything that has happened to me here has helped to spread the Good News.*

If you are dealing with a problem, always see it as an opportunity for showing others how God brings good out of bad circumstances.

EZRA 8:15 | *I found that not one Levite had volunteered to come along.*

Seize any opportunity to volunteer your gifts for God's service.

How do I make the most of opportunities?

JOHN 9:4 | *We must quickly carry out the tasks assigned us by the one who sent us. The night is coming, and then no one can work.*

EPHESIANS 5:16 | *Make the most of every opportunity in these evil days.*

PHILIPPIANS 1:14 | *Because of my imprisonment, most of the believers here have gained confidence and boldly speak God's message without fear.*

When you see an opportunity to do good, jump at it. The more you think about it, the less likely you are to act. Even when you are experiencing personal hardship, helping others can be therapeutic.

GENESIS 39:3-4, 6 | *The LORD was with Joseph, giving him success in everything he did. This pleased Potiphar, so he soon made Joseph his personal attendant. He put him in charge of his entire household and everything he owned. . . . With Joseph there, he didn't worry about a thing.*

GENESIS 41:1, 14, 39-40 | *Later . . . Pharaoh sent for Joseph . . . and he was quickly brought from the prison. . . . Then Pharaoh said to Joseph, "Since God has revealed the meaning of the dreams to you, clearly no one else is as intelligent or wise as you are. You will be in charge of my court, and all my people will take orders from you. Only I, sitting on my throne, will have a rank higher than yours."*

Responsibility will open doors of opportunity. How you handle each responsibility determines whether or not you will be trusted with more. Joseph was unjustly thrown into prison (see Genesis 39:6-20). He could have whined and complained, become bitter and done nothing. Instead, he seized every opportunity he could in his situation, quickly became trusted for his responsibility, and eventually rose to even greater prominence in Egypt.

Promise from God REVELATION 3:8 | *I know all the things you do, and I have opened a door for you that no one can close.*

PARENTING

What does the Bible say about the role of parents?

2 TIMOTHY 3:15 | *You have been taught the holy Scriptures from childhood.*

Parents are to take responsibility for teaching their children a love for the Word of God.

DEUTERONOMY 6:6-7 | *You must commit yourselves wholeheartedly to these commands that I am giving you today. Repeat them again and again to your children. Talk about them when you*

*are at home and when you are on the road, when you are going
to bed and when you are getting up.*

Parents are responsible not only to consistently teach their
children biblical values but to consistently model for them
lives of obedience.

PROVERBS 3:12 | *The LORD corrects those he loves, just as a father
corrects a child in whom he delights.*

HEBREWS 12:11 | *No discipline is enjoyable while it is happen-
ing—it's painful! But afterward there will be a peaceful
harvest of right living.*

Parents are to discipline their children with consistency and
out of love, not anger.

GENESIS 25:28 | *Isaac loved Esau . . . but Rebekah loved Jacob.*

Parents are not to show favoritism between children.

1 SAMUEL 2:29 | *[The Lord said,] "Why do you give your sons
more honor than you give me?"*

Parents are to make sure that God is honored as the head of
the household. Parents do their children a favor when they
sincerely seek what God wants for their children, not necessarily what they want. Indulgent parents do not help their
children develop character.

LUKE 15:20 | *He returned home to his father. And while he was
still a long way off, his father saw him coming. Filled with
love and compassion, he ran to his son, embraced him, and
kissed him.*

The mark of a loving parent is the willingness to forgive.

How are children to relate to their parents?

EXODUS 20:12 | *Honor your father and mother.*

MARK 7:12-13 | *In this way, you let them disregard their needy parents. And so you cancel the word of God in order to hand down your own tradition.*

EPHESIANS 6:1 | *Children, obey your parents because you belong to the Lord, for this is the right thing to do.*

Even if you disagree with your parents, you must show them honor, respect, and obedience.

Promise from God PSALM 127:3 | *Children are a gift from the LORD; they are a reward from him.*

PATIENCE

Is patience really worth working for?

GALATIANS 5:22 | *The Holy Spirit produces this kind of fruit in our lives: love, joy, peace, patience, kindness, goodness, faithfulness.*

COLOSSIANS 1:11 | *We also pray that you will be strengthened with all his glorious power so you will have all the endurance and patience you need. May you be filled with joy.*

Patience leads to endurance to handle difficult circumstances and an expectant attitude of hope that things will get better.

1 CORINTHIANS 13:4, 7 | *Love is patient and kind. . . . Love never gives up, never loses faith, is always hopeful, and endures through every circumstance.*

EPHESIANS 4:2 | *Always be humble and gentle. Be patient with each other, making allowance for each other's faults because of your love.*

Patience is a characteristic of love. The more loving you become, the more you will model the nature of God's patience in your life. God is the perfect example of patience. Every day you fail to measure up to his perfect standard, yet he is slow to get angry and loves you unconditionally.

HEBREWS 10:36 | *Patient endurance is what you need now, so that you will continue to do God's will. Then you will receive all that he has promised.*

Patience is evidence of strong character. As you pass each test of your patience, you will build a higher degree of patience for when you are tested again.

LAMENTATIONS 3:24, 26 | *I say to myself, "The LORD is my inheritance; therefore, I will hope in him!" . . . So it is good to wait quietly for salvation from the LORD.*

JAMES 5:7-8 | *Be patient as you wait for the Lord's return. Consider the farmers who patiently wait for the rains in the fall and in the spring. They eagerly look for the valuable harvest to ripen. You, too, must be patient. Take courage, for the coming of the Lord is near.*

Patience is an important part of faith and hope. The greater your hope, the more you patiently wait, and the more your faith grows.

How do I develop more patience?

JAMES 5:7 | *Consider the farmers who patiently wait for the rains in the fall and in the spring. They eagerly look for the valuable harvest to ripen.*

Whether you're waiting for crops to ripen, a traffic jam to unsnarl, a child to mature, or God to perfect you, you can grow in patience by recognizing that these things take time and there is only so much you can do to help them along.

EXODUS 5:22; 6:2 | *Moses went back to the LORD and protested . . . "Why did you send me?" . . . And God said to Moses, "I am Yahweh—'the LORD.'"*

Focusing less on your agenda and more on God's agenda for you will provide a "big picture" perspective and help you be less impatient.

HABAKKUK 2:3 | *If [the vision] seems slow in coming, wait patiently, for it will surely take place. It will not be delayed.*

Patience can actually give you an attitude of excited anticipation for each new day. If God is going to do what is best for you, then his plan for you will be accomplished on his schedule, not yours. Keeping that in mind, you can actually become excited about waiting for him to act, for you awake each day anticipating what good thing he will work in your life that is just right for you at the present time.

GALATIANS 5:22 | *The Holy Spirit produces this kind of fruit in our lives: love, joy, peace, patience.*

The more you let the Holy Spirit fill and inspire you, the more patient you will become. All fruit takes time to grow and mature, including the fruit of the Holy Spirit.

ROMANS 8:25 | *If we look forward to something we don't yet have, we must wait patiently and confidently.*

Patience is a by-product of the hope a believer has in God's plans, especially his eternal plans. When your long-range future is totally secure, you can be more patient with today's frustrations.

PROVERBS 14:29 | *People with understanding control their anger; a hot temper shows great foolishness.*

2 TIMOTHY 2:24 | *A servant of the Lord must not quarrel but must be kind to everyone, be able to teach, and be patient with difficult people.*

God develops patience in you through your relationships with others. Abrasive relationships teach you to patiently endure. But even in loving relationships, patience is necessary.

1 PETER 2:19-20 | *God is pleased with you when you do what you know is right and patiently endure unfair treatment. Of course, you get no credit for being patient if you are beaten for doing wrong. But if you suffer for doing good and endure it patiently, God is pleased with you.*

God uses life's circumstances to develop your patience. You can't always choose the circumstances that come your way, but you can choose how you will respond to them.

Promise from God   ISAIAH 30:18 | *The LORD must wait for you to come to him so he can show you his love and compassion. For the LORD is a faithful God. Blessed are those who wait for his help.*

PEACE

How can I make peace with God?

PSALM 34:14 | *Turn away from evil and do good. Search for peace, and work to maintain it.*

ROMANS 2:10 | *There will be . . . peace from God for all who do good.*

Peace with God comes from living the way you were created to live. When you admit that you have sinned against him and work toward loving him and loving others by doing good for them, you will experience God's peace as your mind, heart, and actions get in sync with his.

ISAIAH 26:3 | *You will keep in perfect peace all who trust in you, all whose thoughts are fixed on you!*

Peace comes from knowing that God is in control. Focus your thoughts on God and what he is able to accomplish in your life, rather than focusing on your problems.

PSALM 37:11 | *The lowly will possess the land and will live in peace and prosperity.*

MATTHEW 5:5 | *God blesses those who are humble.*

Humility before God brings peace because God blesses the humble. Your humility shows that you understand your place in relation to God and others.

GALATIANS 5:22 | *The Holy Spirit produces this kind of fruit in our lives: . . . peace.*

Let the Holy Spirit fill and rule your life. The Holy Spirit will guide and comfort you. If you follow, learn, and listen, you will experience peace with God.

PSALM 119:165 | *Those who love your instructions have great peace.*

Loving God's Word will give you peace with the God who wrote it.

PHILIPPIANS 4:6-7 | *Don't worry about anything; instead, pray about everything. Tell God what you need, and thank him for all he has done. Then you will experience God's peace.*

Pray about everything. Prayer is indispensable to finding peace with God.

How can I make peace with others?

PSALM 34:14 | *Search for peace, and work to maintain it.*

MATTHEW 5:9 | *God blesses those who work for peace.*

Peace is not the absence of conflict; it's assurance in the midst of conflict. Peace comes from dealing with conflict appropriately.

EPHESIANS 4:3 | *Make every effort to keep yourselves united in the Spirit, binding yourselves together with peace.*

Unity comes from always seeking peace.

PSALM 37:37 | *Look at those who are honest and good, for a wonderful future awaits those who love peace.*

ROMANS 12:17-19 | *Never pay back evil with more evil. . . . Do all that you can to live in peace with everyone. Dear friends, never take revenge. Leave that to . . . God.*

If you harbor thoughts of revenge, you are not at peace with others. Bitterness and revenge can never bring peacefulness.

PROVERBS 12:20 | *Deceit fills hearts that are plotting evil; joy fills hearts that are planning peace!*

Seeking peace with others is one of the surest ways to release streams of joy into your heart.

Promise from God JOHN 14:27 | *[Jesus said,] "I am leaving you with a gift—peace of mind and heart. And the peace I give is a gift the world cannot give. So don't be troubled or afraid."*

PLANNING

How do I go about planning ahead?

ACTS 18:21 | *As [Paul] left, however, he said, "I will come back later, God willing."*

ACTS 22:10 | *[Paul] asked, "What should I do, Lord?" And the Lord told [him], "Get up and go into Damascus, and there you will be told everything you are to do."*

1 PETER 2:19 | *God is pleased with you when you do what you know is right.*

Follow God's revealed will when you make your plans. If his will is not clear in a specific matter, remember that he has made his will clear in general matters of right and wrong, good and bad, helpful and harmful. So you can move ahead with your plans as long as you are confident they do not go against God's Word. As you do, don't be surprised if God intervenes to alter them to let you know his specific will for you.

GENESIS 11:4, 9 | *[The people of the world] said, "Come, let's build a great city for ourselves with a tower that reaches into the sky. This will make us famous and keep us from being scattered all over the world." . . . [But] the LORD confused the people with different languages. In this way he scattered them all over the world.*

PSALM 33:10 | *The LORD frustrates the plans of the nations and thwarts all their schemes.*

Making plans without consulting God to find out what he may want is often a recipe for frustration and disaster.

ROMANS 8:28 | *God causes everything to work together for the good of those who love God and are called according to his purpose for them.*

God will work through your plans, and in spite of them, to accomplish his goals.

JAMES 4:13-16 | *Look here, you who say, "Today or tomorrow we are going to a certain town and will stay there a year. We will do business there and make a profit." How do you know what your life will be like tomorrow? Your life is like the morning fog—it's here a little while, then it's gone. What you ought to say is, "If the Lord wants us to, we will live and do this or that." Otherwise you are boasting about your own plans, and all such boasting is evil.*

Long-range planning is good, but hold those plans loosely. You don't know what the future will bring and where God will take you. So plan ahead, but be flexible as you see God working in your life.

What are some plans I should be making?

PROVERBS 31:15 | *She gets up before dawn to prepare breakfast for her household and plan the day's work for her servant girls.*

The woman in Proverbs 31 is a good example of someone planning her time wisely. Often, making a list of things to accomplish each day can help you stay on track and be productive, avoiding the frustrating feeling that you're wasting time.

1 KINGS 5:5 | *[Solomon said,] "I am planning to build a Temple to honor the name of the LORD my God, just as he had instructed my father, David."*

When God calls you to a specific task, you should make plans to obey. Obedience often requires discipline and sacrifice. How willing are you in these areas?

ROMANS 1:13-14 | *[Paul said,] "I want you to know, dear brothers and sisters, that I planned many times to visit you, but I was prevented until now. I want to work among you and see spiritual fruit, just as I have seen among other Gentiles. For I have a great sense of obligation to people in both the civilized world and the rest of the world, to the educated and uneducated alike."*

Plan to serve and minister to others. In Paul's case, God didn't always put him where he thought he would serve. But Paul continued to make himself available to serve wherever and whomever God chose. As a result, he developed a passion for helping all kinds of people.

1 TIMOTHY 4:14-15 | *Do not neglect the spiritual gift you received through the prophecy spoken over you when the elders of the church laid their hands on you. Give your complete attention to these matters. Throw yourself into your tasks so that everyone will see your progress.*

Plan to exercise your spiritual gifts. Then, make plans to throw yourself into using your abilities to serve God.

HEBREWS 10:25 | *Let us not neglect our meeting together, as some people do, but encourage one another, especially now that the day of his return is drawing near.*

Plan for times of worship and fellowship with other Christians. Don't let the busyness of life cause you to neglect these important times of friendship and encouragement.

JEREMIAH 17:22 | *Do not do your work on the Sabbath, but make it a holy day.*

Plans for hard work are beneficial, but so are plans for times of rest. Work ahead during the week so that you won't feel pressured to work on the Lord's Day. Make it a truly holy day of rest.

1 PETER 5:8 | *Stay alert! Watch out for your great enemy, the devil. He prowls around like a roaring lion, looking for someone to devour.*

Plan ahead to stand firm against temptation. Then, when you are tempted, you will be able to resist and be ready to do the right thing.

MATTHEW 6:19-21 | *Don't store up treasures here on earth, where moths eat them and rust destroys them, and where thieves break in and steal. Store your treasures in heaven. . . . Wherever your treasure is, there the desires of your heart will also be.*

Although it is wise to make plans for your future on earth, it is infinitely wiser to make plans for your eternal future in heaven. Invest in what will last forever.

MATTHEW 25:19-21 | *After a long time their master returned from his trip and called them to give an account of how they had used his money. The servant to whom he had entrusted the five bags of silver came forward with five more and said, "Master, you gave me five bags of silver to invest, and I have earned five more." The master was full of praise. "Well done, my good and faithful servant. You have been faithful in handling this small amount, so now I will give you many more responsibilities."*

Making plans to save and handle your money responsibly is important. Sticking to a regular plan of tithing, saving, and careful spending with what you have now will enable you to handle the responsibilities of greater blessings in the future.

Promise from God PROVERBS 19:21 | *You can make many plans, but the LORD's purpose will prevail.*

PRAISE

For what should I praise God?

1 PETER 1:3 | *All praise to God, the Father of our Lord Jesus Christ. It is by his great mercy that we have been born again, because God raised Jesus Christ from the dead.*

For providing salvation through the death and resurrection of Jesus, his Son.

PSALM 117:1-2 | *Praise the LORD, all you nations. Praise him, all you people of the earth. For he loves us with unfailing love; the LORD's faithfulness endures forever. Praise the LORD!*

For creating you and loving you enough to be your God, inviting you into a personal relationship with him.

PSALM 68:35 | *God is awesome in his sanctuary. The God of Israel gives power and strength to his people. Praise be to God!*

PSALM 77:13 | *O God, your ways are holy. Is there any god as mighty as you?*

For his holiness and awesome power.

PSALM 106:1 | *Praise the LORD! Give thanks to the LORD, for he is good! His faithful love endures forever.*

For his faithful and unfailing love for you.

PSALM 28:6 | *Praise the LORD! For he has heard my cry for mercy.*

2 CORINTHIANS 1:3 | *All praise to God, the Father of our Lord Jesus Christ. God is our merciful Father and the source of all comfort.*

For his mercy despite your sinfulness.

DANIEL 2:20 | *Praise the name of God forever and ever, for he has all wisdom and power.*

For his wisdom that is far beyond what you can know or understand, which he makes available to you in every situation.

PSALM 139:9-10 | *If I ride the wings of the morning, if I dwell by the farthest oceans, even there your hand will guide me, and your strength will support me.*

For his guidance in your life.

PSALM 119:108, 111 | *LORD, accept my offering of praise, and teach me your regulations. . . . Your laws are my treasure; they are my heart's delight.*

For giving you his Word as truth to live by.

PSALM 107:8 | *Let them praise the LORD for his great love and for the wonderful things he has done for them.*

ISAIAH 25:1 | *O LORD, I will honor and praise your name, for you are my God. You do such wonderful things! You planned them long ago, and now you have accomplished them.*

For what he has done for you and for all his people.

Promise from God 2 THESSALONIANS 1:10 | *When he comes on that day, he will receive glory from his holy people—praise from all who believe. And this includes you, for you believed what we told you about him.*

PRAYER

What is prayer?

2 CHRONICLES 7:14 | *[The Lord said,] "If my people who are called by my name will humble themselves and pray and seek my face and turn from their wicked ways, I will hear from heaven."*

PSALM 140:6 | *I said to the LORD, "You are my God!" Listen, O LORD, to my cries for mercy!*

Prayer is conversation with God. It is simply talking with God and listening to him, honestly telling him your thoughts and feelings, praising him, thanking him, confessing sin, and asking for his help and advice. The essence of prayer is humbly entering the very presence of almighty God.

PSALM 38:18 | *I confess my sins; I am deeply sorry for what I have done.*

1 JOHN 1:9 | *If we confess our sins to him, he is faithful and just to forgive us our sins and to cleanse us.*

Prayer often begins with a confession of sin. It is through confession that you demonstrate the humility necessary for open lines of communication with the almighty, holy God.

1 SAMUEL 14:36 | *The priest said, "Let's ask God first."*

2 SAMUEL 5:19 | *David asked the LORD, "Should I go out to fight the Philistines?"*

Prayer is asking God for guidance and waiting for his direction and leading.

MARK 1:35 | *Before daybreak the next morning, Jesus got up and went out to an isolated place to pray.*

Prayer is an expression of an intimate relationship with your heavenly Father, who makes his own love and resources available to you. Just as you enjoy being with people you love, you enjoy spending time with God the more you get to know him and understand just how much he loves you.

1 SAMUEL 3:10 | *The LORD came and called as before, "Samuel! Samuel!" And Samuel replied, "Speak, your servant is listening."*

Good conversation also includes listening, so make time for God to speak to you. When you listen to God, he will make his wisdom known to you.

PSALM 9:1-2 | *I will praise you, LORD, with all my heart; I will tell of all the marvelous things you have done. I will be filled with joy because of you. I will sing praises to your name, O Most High.*

Through prayer you praise your mighty God.

Does the Bible teach a "right" way to pray?

1 SAMUEL 23:2 | *David asked the LORD, "Should I go . . . ?"*

NEHEMIAH 1:4 | *For days I mourned, fasted, and prayed to the God of heaven.*

PSALM 18:1 | *I love you, LORD; you are my strength.*

PSALM 32:5 | *Finally, I confessed all my sins to you and stopped trying to hide my guilt. I said to myself, "I will confess my rebellion to the LORD." And you forgave me! All my guilt is gone.*

EPHESIANS 6:18 | *Pray in the Spirit at all times and on every occasion. Stay alert and be persistent in your prayers for all believers everywhere.*

Throughout the Bible effective prayer includes elements of adoration, fasting, confession, petition, and persistence.

MATTHEW 6:9-13 | *[Jesus said,] "Pray like this: Our Father in heaven, may your name be kept holy. May your Kingdom come soon. May your will be done on earth, as it is in heaven. Give us today the food we need, and forgive us our sins, as we have forgiven those who sin against us. And don't let us yield to temptation, but rescue us from the evil one."*

Jesus taught his disciples that prayer is an intimate relationship with the Father that includes a dependency for daily needs, a commitment to obedience, and forgiveness of sin.

NEHEMIAH 2:4-5 | *The king asked, "Well, how can I help you?" With a [quick] prayer to the God of heaven, I replied.*

Prayer can be spontaneous.

Does God always answer prayer?

PSALM 116:1-2 | *I love the LORD because he hears my voice and my prayer for mercy. Because he bends down to listen, I will pray as long as I have breath!*

1 PETER 3:12 | *The eyes of the Lord watch over those who do right, and his ears are open to their prayers. But the Lord turns his face against those who do evil.*

God listens carefully to every prayer and answers it. His answer may be yes, no, or wait. Any loving parent gives all three of these responses to a child. God's answering yes to every request would spoil you and be dangerous to your well-being. Answering no to every request would be vindictive, stingy, and damaging to your spirit. Answering wait to every prayer would be frustrating. God always answers based on what he knows is best for you.

JAMES 5:16 | *The earnest prayer of a righteous person has great power and produces wonderful results.*

1 JOHN 5:14-15 | *He hears us whenever we ask for anything that pleases him. And . . . he will give us what we ask for.*

As you maintain a close relationship with Jesus and consistently study his Word, your prayers will be more aligned with his will. When that happens, God is delighted to grant your requests.

2 CORINTHIANS 12:8-9 | *Three different times [Paul] begged the Lord to take [the thorn in his flesh] away. Each time he said, "My grace is all you need. My power works best in weakness."*

Sometimes, like Paul, you will find that God answers prayer by giving you something better than you asked for.

JOHN 14:14 | *[Jesus said,] "Ask me for anything in my name, and I will do it!"*

Jesus' name is not a magic wand. Praying in Jesus' name means praying according to Jesus' character and purposes. When you pray like this, you are asking for what God already wants to give you.

EXODUS 14:15 | *The LORD said to Moses, "Why are you crying out to me? Tell the people to get moving!"*

Effective prayer is accompanied by a willingness to obey. When God opens a door, walk through it!

Promise from God PSALM 145:18 | *The LORD is close to all who call on him, yes, to all who call on him in truth.*

PREJUDICE

What does the Bible say about ethnic or racial prejudice?

LUKE 10:33 | *A despised Samaritan came along, and when he saw the man, he felt compassion for him.*

JOHN 4:9 | *The woman was surprised, for Jews refuse to have anything to do with Samaritans. She said to Jesus, "You are a Jew, and I am a Samaritan woman. Why are you asking me for a drink?"*

ACTS 10:28 | *Peter [said], "You know it is against our laws for a Jewish man to enter a Gentile home like this or to associate with you. But God has shown me that I should no longer think of anyone as impure or unclean."*

Jesus broke the judgmental stereotypes of his time. He reached across lines of racial and gender prejudice and division to demonstrate equality and respect for all people. God made us all different so that when we work together our efforts are more complete, more beautiful, and more effective for everyone. There are few things more powerful and productive than a diverse group of people working in unity.

What are other areas in which the Bible warns you not to be prejudiced?

1 SAMUEL 16:7 | *The LORD said to Samuel, "Don't judge by his appearance or height. . . . The LORD doesn't see things the way you see them. People judge by outward appearance, but the LORD looks at the heart."*

ISAIAH 53:2 | *My servant grew up in the LORD's presence like a tender green shoot, like a root in dry ground. There was nothing beautiful or majestic about his appearance, nothing to attract us to him.*

Appearance. Stereotypes abound—prejudice against all kinds of people. But the real person is inside; the body is only the shell, the temporary housing. It is wrong to judge a person by outward appearance; the real person inside may be a person of incredible beauty. Even Jesus may not have had the tall, handsome body often attributed to him, for Isaiah the prophet said about the coming Savior, "There was nothing beautiful or majestic about his appearance."

PROVERBS 14:20-21 | *The poor are despised even by their neighbors, while the rich have many "friends." It is a sin to belittle one's neighbor; blessed are those who help the poor.*

JAMES 2:3-4 | *If you give special attention and a good seat to the rich person, but you say to the poor one, "You can stand over there, or else sit on the floor"—well, doesn't this discrimination show that your judgments are guided by evil motives?*

Economic status. A wealthy person and a poor person come to church. Who is welcomed more? A wealthy person and a poor person speak up in a church committee meeting. Which one do you listen to most carefully?

MATTHEW 18:10 | *[Jesus said,] "Beware that you don't look down on any of these little ones. For I tell you that in heaven their angels are always in the presence of my heavenly Father."*

1 TIMOTHY 4:12 | *Don't let anyone think less of you because you are young.*

1 TIMOTHY 5:1 | *Never speak harshly to an older man, but appeal to him respectfully as you would to your own father.*

Age. To youth belongs the future; to old age belongs the honor of accomplishment. Youth has the opportunity to win the world; old age has the experience of victory. Each should be honored for its contributions.

MARK 6:2-3 | *[Those who heard Jesus' teaching] asked, "Where did he get all this wisdom and the power to perform such miracles?" Then they scoffed, "He's just a carpenter, the son of Mary." . . . They were deeply offended and refused to believe in him.*

Occupation. God does not write off families or occupations, and perhaps that is why Jesus chose to come to the family of a carpenter rather than to the family of a king. God loves each person, regardless of occupation.

JOHN 1:46 | *"Nazareth!" exclaimed Nathanael. "Can anything good come from Nazareth?"*

Location. You must not be prejudiced because of where a person grew up. The "other side of the tracks" is often viewed negatively, but God lives on both sides of the tracks.

Is the world prejudiced against Christ's followers?

JOHN 15:19 | *[Jesus said,] "The world would love you as one of its own if you belonged to it, but you are no longer part of the world. I chose you to come out of the world, so it hates you."*

Those who don't know Christ often enjoy sin and want to persist in it, so it's natural for them to be opposed to Jesus' teachings and his followers.

Promise from God COLOSSIANS 3:14 | *Above all, clothe yourselves with love, which binds us all together in perfect harmony.*

PRIDE

Why is pride considered one of the "seven deadly sins"?

EZEKIEL 28:17 | *Your heart was filled with pride because of all your beauty.*

The Bible seems to indicate that pride is the sin that resulted in Lucifer's (Satan's) being cast from heaven (see Ezekiel 28:13-17). If selfish pride is strong enough to rip an angel away from the very presence of God in heaven, it is certainly strong enough to do much damage in your own life.

DANIEL 5:20 | *When his heart and mind were puffed up with arrogance, he was brought down from his royal throne and stripped of his glory.*

Pride leads to hardness of heart, which in turn leads to an arrogant disregard of God and sin.

PSALM 10:4 | *The wicked are too proud to seek God. They seem to think that God is dead.*

Pride leads to ignoring God (because you think your way is better) and setting a course for a life of disobedience.

2 TIMOTHY 3:2-4 | *They will be boastful and proud, . . . unloving and unforgiving. . . . They will betray their friends.*

Pride can destroy your relationships faster than almost anything else because it uses others to strengthen your position at their expense.

LUKE 18:11 | *The Pharisee stood by himself and prayed this prayer: "I thank you, God, that I am not a sinner like everyone else. . . . I'm certainly not like that tax collector!"*

Pride blinds you to your own sin.

OBADIAH 1:3 | *You have been deceived by your own pride because you live in a rock fortress and make your home high in the mountains. "Who can ever reach us way up here?" you ask boastfully.*

Pride finds comfort in false security.

ACTS 8:30-31 | *Philip ran over and heard the man reading from the prophet Isaiah. Philip asked, "Do you understand what you are reading?" The man replied, "How can I, unless someone instructs me?" And he urged Philip to come up into the carriage and sit with him.*

Pride keeps you from asking others for help. In this case, the man in the carriage had the humility to ask for help.

Is pride ever healthy or appropriate?

ROMANS 15:17 | *[Paul said,] "I have reason to be enthusiastic about all Christ Jesus has done through me in my service to God."*

You can feel satisfaction in what God does through you. Paul was proud, not of what he had accomplished on his own but of what God had accomplished through him.

2 CORINTHIANS 5:12-13 | *Are we commending ourselves to you again? No, we are giving you a reason to be proud of us, so you can answer those who brag about having a spectacular ministry rather than having a sincere heart. If it seems we are crazy, it is to bring glory to God.*

If you take pride in anything, you ought to take pride in the God you serve.

1 CORINTHIANS 1:30-31 | *Christ made us right with God; he made us pure and holy, and he freed us from sin. Therefore, as the Scriptures say, "If you want to boast, boast only about the LORD."*

Pride is appropriate when it causes you to be grateful to God for his gifts. When you look at your spouse, or children, or talents and your heart wells up with gratitude to God, he is pleased. Then your focus is on him and not on yourself.

Promise from God PROVERBS 16:18 | *Pride goes before destruction, and haughtiness before a fall.*

PRIORITIES

How do I know what's really important?

1 SAMUEL 14:35 | *Saul built an altar to the LORD; it was the first of the altars he built to the LORD.*

Don't confuse what's urgent with what's important. This verse, taken out of context, makes it sound like Saul's greatest priority was worshiping God. But Saul finally got around to building an altar to God months and possibly years after he was first anointed king. That which seemed urgent had taken him away from where he really needed to be spending his time—worshiping God.

MARK 10:31 | *Many who are the greatest now will be least important then, and those who seem least important now will be the greatest then.*

If all your priorities focus on what you think is best for you, you will not achieve God's best for you. Always seek God's input first in any decision. When considering some course of action, ask yourself if it would be God's priority for you.

HAGGAI 1:9 | *You hoped for rich harvests, but they were poor. And when you brought your harvest home, I blew it away. Why? Because my house lies in ruins, says the LORD of Heaven's Armies, while all of you are busy building your own fine houses.*

Priorities are scales on which your love for God is weighed. Be sure to take care of God's agenda before your own.

How do I set priorities?

DEUTERONOMY 10:12-13 | *What does the LORD your God require of you? He requires only that you fear the LORD your God, and live in a way that pleases him, and love him and serve him with all your heart and soul. And you must always obey the LORD's commands.*

JOSHUA 24:15 | *Choose today whom you will serve. . . . As for me and my family, we will serve the LORD.*

JOHN 3:16 | *God loved the world so much that he gave his one and only Son, so that everyone who believes in him will not perish but have eternal life.*

There is no higher priority than loving and obeying God and accepting Jesus' gift of salvation. Nothing affects your eternal future so significantly, and nothing will alter your immediate future so significantly.

PROVERBS 3:5-6 | *Trust in the LORD with all your heart; do not depend on your own understanding. Seek his will in all you do, and he will show you which path to take.*

Not only is putting God first in your life your top priority, but it helps put all your other priorities in order as well.

1 KINGS 3:9 | *Give me an understanding heart so that I can . . . know the difference between right and wrong.*

Tenaciously seeking after God's wisdom is the way to discern right priorities.

1 SAMUEL 14:36 | *Saul said, "Let's chase the Philistines all night and plunder them until sunrise. Let's destroy every last one of them." His men replied, "We'll do whatever you think is best." But the priest said, "Let's ask God first."*

Get God's input before setting your priorities.

MATTHEW 6:33 | *Seek the Kingdom of God above all else, and live righteously, and he will give you everything you need.*

Be intentional about your priorities. Set them and tend to them first. Only then will your life have its fullest meaning.

ECCLESIASTES 2:11 | *As I looked at everything I had worked so hard to accomplish, it was all so meaningless—like chasing the wind.*

LUKE 10:40-42 | *Martha was distracted by the big dinner she was preparing. She came to Jesus and said, "Lord, doesn't it seem unfair to you that my sister just sits here while I do all the work? Tell her to come and help me." But the Lord said to her, "My dear Martha, you are worried and upset over all these details! There is only one thing worth being concerned about. Mary has discovered it, and it will not be taken away from her."*

If you make spending time with the Lord your first priority of the day, you will find that he will give you perspective on your activities for the rest of the day. Ask God to show you what is worth being concerned about.

What happens when we fail to set the right priorities?

JUDGES 17:6 | *In those days Israel had no king; all the people did whatever seemed right in their own eyes.*

When you do whatever seems right to you rather than setting right priorities, you will stop doing what is right in God's eyes.

Promise from God   PROVERBS 3:5-6 | *Trust in the LORD with all your heart; do not depend on your own understanding. Seek his will in all you do, and he will show you which path to take.*

PURPOSE

Does God have a special purpose for me?

PSALM 57:2 | *I cry out to God Most High, to God who will fulfill his purpose for me.*

God has a general purpose and a specific purpose for you. Your general purpose is to let the love of Jesus shine through you to make an impact on others. More specifically, God has given you spiritual gifts (see Romans 12:6-8; 1 Corinthians 12:4-11; 1 Peter 4:10-11) and wants you to use them to make a unique contribution in your sphere of influence. The better you fulfill your general purpose, the clearer your specific purpose will become.

ACTS 20:24 | *My life is worth nothing to me unless I use it for finishing the work assigned me by the Lord Jesus—the work of telling others the Good News about the wonderful grace of God.*

Part of God's purpose for you is to bring his Good News of salvation to others who need to know it.

2 TIMOTHY 1:9 | *God saved us and called us to live a holy life. He did this, not because we deserved it, but because that was his plan from before the beginning of time—to show us his grace through Christ Jesus.*

You are called by God to live a holy life and to show the love of Jesus to others by the way you live.

How can I discover God's specific purpose for me and fulfill it?

ROMANS 12:1-2 | *Give your bodies to God because of all he has done for you. Let them be a living and holy sacrifice—the kind he will find acceptable. . . . Don't copy the behavior and customs of this world, but let God transform you into a new person by changing the way you think. Then you will learn to know God's will for you, which is good and pleasing and perfect.*

Discovering God's purpose for you begins with your whole-hearted commitment to God. He promises to make his will known to you as you make yourself available to him.

1 SAMUEL 17:26 | *David asked the soldiers . . . "Who is this pagan Philistine anyway, that he is allowed to defy the armies of the living God?"*

While others saw a fearsome giant, David saw an opportunity for God's mighty work, and his purpose therefore became clear (see 1 Samuel 17:32, 50). Don't let obstacles stop you from discovering the purpose God has for you.

NEHEMIAH 2:17 | *Let us rebuild the wall of Jerusalem and end this disgrace!*

Nehemiah's passion to rebuild the walls of Jerusalem was rooted in understanding what God wanted for his people. Passionately pursue the process of discovering what God wants for you.

PHILIPPIANS 1:20 | *[Paul said,] "I fully expect and hope . . . that I will continue to be bold for Christ. . . . And I trust that my life will bring honor to Christ, whether I live or die."*

PHILIPPIANS 3:12 | *[Paul said,] "I don't mean to say that I have already achieved these things or that I have already reached perfection. But I press on to possess that perfection for which Christ Jesus first possessed me."*

Paul's great purpose, whether by life or by death, was to win others to Christ. Your purpose will be something you feel compelled to do regardless of the risks.

ACTS 13:2 | *One day as these men were worshiping the Lord and fasting, the Holy Spirit said, "Dedicate Barnabas and Saul for the special work to which I have called them."*

Worshiping, praying, fasting, and participating in relationships with other believers will help you discern God's purpose for your life.

Promise from God PSALM 57:2 | *I cry out to God Most High, to God who will fulfill his purpose for me.*

REGRETS

How can I deal with regrets in my life?

2 CORINTHIANS 5:17 | *Anyone who belongs to Christ has become a new person. The old life is gone; a new life has begun!*

When you come to faith in Jesus, he forgives your sins—all of them. Your past is forgotten to him, and he gives you a fresh start. You will still have to live with the consequences of your sins because they cannot be retracted. But because God forgives you, you can move forward without the tremendous guilt that can accompany regret.

PSALM 31:10 | *I am dying from grief; my years are shortened by sadness. Sin has drained my strength; I am wasting away from within.*

PHILIPPIANS 3:13 | *I focus on this one thing: Forgetting the past and looking forward to what lies ahead.*

Focus on God, who controls the future, not on regrets of the past. God doesn't cause regrets; he washes them away when you ask him to walk with you into the future.

MATTHEW 16:18 | *[Jesus said,] "Now I say to you that you are Peter (which means 'rock'), and upon this rock I will build my church, and all the powers of hell will not conquer it."*

MATTHEW 26:73-75 | *Some of the other bystanders came over to Peter and said, "You must be one of them; we can tell by your Galilean accent." Peter swore, "A curse on me if I'm lying— I don't know the man!" And immediately the rooster crowed. Suddenly, Jesus' words flashed through Peter's mind: "Before the rooster crows, you will deny three times that you even know me." And he went away, weeping bitterly.*

GALATIANS 2:7-9 | *God had given . . . Peter the responsibility of preaching to the Jews. . . . God . . . worked through Peter as the apostle to the Jews. . . . In fact, James, Peter, and John . . . were known as pillars of the church.*

Turn your regrets into resolve. Regrets can be so powerful that they disable you from serving God in the future. If Peter had focused on his regret over denying Jesus, he would never have been able to preach the Good News about Jesus so powerfully. Don't let regret paralyze you; instead, let it motivate you to positive action for God in the future.

PSALM 30:11 | *You have turned my mourning into joyful dancing. You have taken away my clothes of mourning and clothed me with joy.*

PSALM 51:12 | *Restore to me the joy of your salvation, and make me willing to obey you.*

Let your regrets draw you closer to God. Don't let them pull you away from God. He wants to take your burdens from you and restore your relationships with him and others. Don't cause the biggest regret of your life—withdrawing from God. No matter what you've done, he welcomes you with loving arms.

ROMANS 8:28 | *God causes everything to work together for the good of those who love God and are called according to his purpose for them.*

Remember that God has the ability to turn bad into good. He can use even the things you regret to accomplish his will.

1 CHRONICLES 21:8 | *David said to God, "I have sinned greatly by taking this census. Please forgive my guilt for doing this foolish thing."*

MATTHEW 18:21-22 | *Peter came to [Jesus] and asked, "Lord, how often should I forgive someone who sins against me? Seven times?" "No, not seven times," Jesus replied, "but seventy times seven!"*

LUKE 15:18 | *I will go home to my father and say, "Father, I have sinned against both heaven and you."*

Sin always brings regret because it damages the relationships most important to you. Whether it is your own sin or the sin of someone against you, sin causes a deep rift in a relationship; now you are facing conflict, separation, loneliness, frustration, anger, and other kinds of emotions. Forgiveness—whether confessing your sin to God and others or granting forgiveness to others—is the only way to give your heart a chance to start over. It doesn't take away past regrets, but it changes your perspective from regret to restoration. It keeps you focused on the healing that can happen in the future rather than on the wounds that you caused (or received) in the past.

In the future, how can I avoid regrets?

MATTHEW 7:12 | *Do to others whatever you would like them to do to you. This is the essence of all that is taught in the law and the prophets.*

When you treat others the way you like to be treated, you will have no regrets.

2 CORINTHIANS 1:12 | *We can say with confidence and a clear conscience that we have lived with a God-given holiness and sincerity in all our dealings.*

1 PETER 3:15-17 | *You must worship Christ as Lord of your life. And if someone asks about your Christian hope, always be ready to explain it. But do this in a gentle and respectful way. Keep your conscience clear. Then if people speak against you, they will be ashamed when they see what a good life you live because you belong to Christ. Remember, it is better to suffer*

for doing good, if that is what God wants, than to suffer for doing wrong!

Follow your conscience and always do what is right. This will keep you from getting into situations you will later regret.

MATTHEW 27:3 | *When Judas, who had betrayed [Jesus], realized that Jesus had been condemned to die, he was filled with remorse.*

Thinking through the full consequences of your decisions in advance will keep you from making decisions you will later regret.

1 THESSALONIANS 5:22 | *Stay away from every kind of evil.*

Stay away from the places and people who tempt you to sin, and you will have less to regret.

PSALM 1:1-2 | *Oh, the joys of those who do not follow the advice of the wicked, or stand around with sinners, or join in with mockers. But they delight in the law of the LORD, meditating on it day and night.*

Immerse yourself in Scripture and surround yourself with positive influences who will give you good advice.

PROVERBS 14:29 | *People with understanding control their anger; a hot temper shows great foolishness.*

Avoid acting on impulse in the heat of anger. A hasty mistake has lasting effects.

EXODUS 23:2-3 | *Do not be swayed by the crowd to twist justice. And do not slant your testimony in favor of a person.*

Don't let your peers pressure you into doing something you know is foolish or sinful.

PROVERBS 15:1 | *A gentle answer deflects anger, but harsh words make tempers flare.*

JAMES 3:2, 5 | *If we could control our tongues, we . . . could also control ourselves in every other way. . . . The tongue is a small thing that makes grand speeches. But a tiny spark can set a great forest on fire.*

The greatest regrets are often caused by words; once spoken they cannot be taken back. If you have even a hint that you might regret what you are about to say, don't speak.

Promise from God 2 CORINTHIANS 7:10 | *The kind of sorrow God wants us to experience leads us away from sin and results in salvation. There's no regret for that kind of sorrow.*

REJECTION

How can I recover from rejection in my life?

ISAIAH 53:3 | *He was despised and rejected. . . . We turned our backs on him and looked the other way.*

You have a Savior who understands rejection because he was despised, rejected, and killed by his own family, community, and nation. Find comfort in your relationship with a God who understands what you are going through.

JOHN 14:26 | *When the Father sends the Advocate as my representative—that is, the Holy Spirit—he will teach you everything and will remind you of everything I have told you.*

ACTS 9:31 | *The church then had peace . . . and it became stronger as the believers lived in the fear of the Lord. And with the encouragement of the Holy Spirit, it also grew.*

If you believe in Jesus, he promises that the Holy Spirit will stay with you forever. Listen to the Spirit's voice of comfort, compassion, and encouragement.

MARK 6:4 | *Jesus [said], "A prophet is honored everywhere except in his own hometown and among his relatives and his own family."*

Rejection by others does not change your value or the truth about yourself. Jesus was God's Son regardless of his rejection or acceptance by mankind. Instead of focusing on what other people think about you, focus on God's love for you.

LUKE 6:22-23 | *What blessings await you when people hate you and exclude you and mock you and curse you as evil because you follow the Son of Man. When that happens, be happy! Yes, leap for joy! For a great reward awaits you in heaven. And remember, their ancestors treated the ancient prophets that same way.*

ACTS 5:41 | *The apostles left the high council rejoicing that God had counted them worthy to suffer disgrace for the name of Jesus.*

If you are rejected for being a Christian, rejoice and persevere because you will receive special blessings from God.

Will God ever reject me?

JOHN 4:10 | *Jesus replied [to the Samaritan woman], "If you only knew the gift God has for you and who you are speaking to, you would ask me, and I would give you living water."*

Jesus did not reject the sinful Samaritan woman, but rather he showed her acceptance by offering her living water. Jesus will never reject anyone who comes to him to be cleansed from sin.

JOHN 8:10-11 | *"Didn't even one of them condemn you?" "No, Lord," she said. And Jesus said, "Neither do I. Go and sin no more."*

God rejects the sin without rejecting the sinner.

JOHN 6:37 | *[Jesus said,] "Those the Father has given me will come to me, and I will never reject them."*

God accepts all who come to him in faith, even those who previously rejected him.

ISAIAH 55:3, 6 | *[The Lord says,] "Come to me with your ears wide open. Listen, and you will find life. I will make an everlasting covenant with you. I will give you all the unfailing love I promised to David." . . . Seek the LORD while you can find him. Call on him now while he is near.*

Don't misinterpret God's silence as rejection. When God seems silent, it is often because you are too busy to hear him. Or it might be that he is being quiet so that you will draw closer to him in order to more fully experience his love and acceptance.

Promise from God HEBREWS 13:5 | *God has said, "I will never fail you. I will never abandon you."*

REPENTANCE

What is repentance?

MATTHEW 3:2 | *Repent of your sins and turn to God, for the Kingdom of Heaven is near.*

MATTHEW 16:24 | *Jesus said to his disciples, "If any of you wants to be my follower, you must turn from your selfish ways, take up your cross, and follow me."*

Repentance means being sorry for sin and being committed to a new way of life—that of serving God. It means turning from a life that is ruled by your sinful nature and turning to God for a new nature, which comes when God's Spirit begins to live in you.

PSALM 32:3-5 | *When I refused to confess my sin, my body wasted away, and I groaned all day long. Day and night your hand of discipline was heavy on me. My strength evaporated like water in the summer heat. Finally, I confessed all my sins to you and stopped trying to hide my guilt. I said to myself, "I will confess my rebellion to the LORD." And you forgave me! All my guilt is gone.*

1 JOHN 1:9-10 | *If we confess our sins to him, he is faithful and just to forgive us our sins and to cleanse us from all wickedness. If we claim we have not sinned, we are calling God a liar and showing that his word has no place in our hearts.*

One of the first essential steps to repentance is confession, which means being humbly honest with God and sincerely sorry for your sins—the ones you know about and the ones you are unaware of. Confession restores your relationship with God, and this renews your strength and spirit. When you repent, God removes your guilt, restores your joy, and heals your broken soul. A heart that truly longs for change is necessary for repentance to be genuine.

Why is repentance necessary?

ROMANS 3:23 | *Everyone has sinned; we all fall short of God's glorious standard.*

Repentance is necessary because every person ever born has sinned against God and betrayed him.

2 CHRONICLES 30:9 | *The LORD your God is gracious and merciful. If you return to him, he will not continue to turn his face from you.*

JEREMIAH 3:22 | *"My wayward children," says the LORD, "come back to me, and I will heal your wayward hearts." "Yes, we're coming," the people reply, "for you are the LORD our God."*

Repentance is necessary for an ongoing relationship with God. Turn away from anything that is preventing you from worshiping and obeying God wholeheartedly.

JEREMIAH 3:12 | *This is what the LORD says: "O Israel, my faithless people, come home to me again, for I am merciful. I will not be angry with you forever."*

1 TIMOTHY 1:16 | *God had mercy on me so that Christ Jesus could use me as a prime example of his great patience with even*

the worst sinners. Then others will realize that they, too, can believe in him and receive eternal life.

Repentance is your only hope of receiving God's mercy. Those who refuse to see and admit their own sins can't be forgiven for them and have placed themselves outside God's mercy and blessing.

2 CORINTHIANS 5:17 | *Anyone who belongs to Christ has become a new person. The old life is gone; a new life has begun!*

GALATIANS 2:20 | *My old self has been crucified with Christ. It is no longer I who live, but Christ lives in me.*

TITUS 3:5 | *[God] saved us, not because of the righteous things we had done, but because of his mercy. He washed away our sins, giving us a new birth and new life through the Holy Spirit.*

Repentance allows you to receive a new life from God; literally, a life where the very Spirit of God lives within you.

LUKE 24:47 | *There is forgiveness of sins for all who repent.*

Repentance allows you to receive forgiveness of sin. If you are sincere when you come to God and ask him humbly, he will forgive your sin.

Is repentance a one-time event, or do I need to repent each time I sin?

PSALM 51:17 | *The sacrifice you desire is a broken spirit. You will not reject a broken and repentant heart, O God.*

While salvation is a one-time event, God is pleased by broken and contrite hearts that are willing to continually confess and repent of sin.

1 JOHN 1:8-9 | *If we claim we have no sin, we are only fooling ourselves and not living in the truth. But if we confess our sins to him, he is faithful and just to forgive us.*

Confessing and repenting of sin are daily habits of the person walking in the light of fellowship with God.

Promise from God ACTS 2:38 | *Each of you must repent of your sins and turn to God, and be baptized in the name of Jesus Christ for the forgiveness of your sins. Then you will receive the gift of the Holy Spirit.*

REPUTATION

How can I cultivate and maintain a godly reputation?

PROVERBS 3:1-2 | *My child, never forget the things I have taught you. Store my commands in your heart. If you do this, . . . your life will be satisfying.*

Following God's direction in Scripture is the essential ingredient in developing a godly reputation.

PROVERBS 3:3-4 | *Never let loyalty and kindness leave you! Tie them around your neck as a reminder. Write them deep within your heart. Then you will find favor with both God and people, and you will earn a good reputation.*

God promises to give you a good name when you show kindness, loyalty, and love to people.

PROVERBS 22:1 | *Choose a good reputation over great riches; being held in high esteem is better than silver or gold.*

God blesses your reputation when you resist the temptation to trade your good name and honor for wealth.

ROMANS 14:17-18 | *The Kingdom of God is not a matter of what we eat or drink, but of living a life of goodness and peace and joy in the Holy Spirit. If you serve Christ with this attitude, you will please God, and others will approve of you, too.*

PHILIPPIANS 4:4-5 | *Always be full of joy in the Lord. I say it again—rejoice! Let everyone see that you are considerate in all you do.*

Focusing less on insignificant, external behaviors and more on internal character will please God, and ultimately it will gain the approval of others, too.

GALATIANS 5:22-23 | *The Holy Spirit produces this kind of fruit in our lives: love, joy, peace, patience, kindness, goodness, faithfulness, gentleness, and self-control.*

People often argue that their personal lives do not matter as long as they perform well on the job or look good in public. God, however, does not make a distinction between public and private life. Justice, righteousness, integrity, mercy, honesty, fairness, and faithfulness are essential traits of a person's character and reputation because they reflect God's character. You will have a good reputation when you display the same godly integrity in private as you do in public.

How can a bad reputation be changed?

1 PETER 2:11-12 | *Dear friends, I warn you as "temporary residents and foreigners" to keep away from worldly desires that wage war against your very souls. Be careful to live properly*

among your . . . neighbors. Then . . . they will see your honorable behavior, and they will give honor to God.

The surest way to influence how others think of you is by consistent, godly behavior.

ROMANS 12:2 | *Don't copy the behavior and customs of this world, but let God transform you into a new person by changing the way you think. Then you will learn to know God's will for you, which is good and pleasing and perfect.*

Jesus' love can transform you, and eventually your reputation will change too.

How can I keep from damaging the reputation of others?

PROVERBS 25:10 | *Others may accuse you of gossip, and you will never regain your good reputation.*

Refrain from gossip, which robs other people of their reputation by taking away their integrity. With a single sentence you can ruin the reputation of others. By gossiping, you will damage your reputation as well.

Promise from God PROVERBS 22:1 | *Choose a good reputation over great riches; being held in high esteem is better than silver or gold.*

RESPECT

How do I gain respect?

1 KINGS 13:8 | *The man of God said to the king, "Even if you gave me half of everything you own, I would not go with you."*

MATTHEW 7:12 | *Do to others whatever you would like them to do to you.*

JUDE 1:20 | *You, dear friends, must build each other up in your most holy faith [and] pray in the power of the Holy Spirit.*

You gain respect in much the same way you give it—by building your life on God's Word, treating others the way you would like to be treated, standing up for truth no matter what, and not compromising your character.

How do I show respect for God?

DEUTERONOMY 10:12 | *What does the LORD your God require of you? He requires only that you fear the LORD your God, and live in a way that pleases him, and love him and serve him with all your heart and soul.*

HEBREWS 12:28-29 | *Since we are receiving a Kingdom that is unshakable, let us be thankful and please God by worshiping him with holy fear and awe. For our God is a devouring fire.*

Worshiping and revering God are demonstrations of your respect for him.

1 CHRONICLES 16:8-10 | *Give thanks to the LORD and proclaim his greatness. Let the whole world know what he has done. Sing to him; yes, sing his praises. Tell everyone about his wonderful deeds. Exult in his holy name; rejoice, you who worship the LORD.*

PSALM 22:23 | *Praise the LORD, all you who fear him! Honor him, all you descendants of Jacob! Show him reverence, all you descendants of Israel!*

Praising God for who he is and what he has done shows respect for him.

PSALM 62:5 | *Let all that I am wait quietly before God, for my hope is in him.*

ECCLESIASTES 5:1 | *As you enter the house of God, keep your ears open and your mouth shut.*

ZEPHANIAH 1:7 | *Stand in silence in the presence of the Sovereign LORD.*

Being silent long enough to listen to God shows that you respect him enough to come to him for direction.

How can I show respect to others?

LUKE 10:33-34 | *A despised Samaritan came along, and when he saw the man, he felt compassion for him. Going over to him, the Samaritan soothed his wounds with olive oil and wine and bandaged them. Then he put the man on his own donkey and took him to an inn, where he took care of him.*

ROMANS 12:10 | *Love each other with genuine affection, and take delight in honoring each other.*

ROMANS 13:7 | *Give to everyone what you owe them . . . , and give respect and honor to those who are in authority.*

PHILIPPIANS 2:3 | *Don't be selfish; don't try to impress others. Be humble, thinking of others as better than yourselves.*

JAMES 2:1 | *My dear brothers and sisters, how can you claim to have faith in our glorious Lord Jesus Christ if you favor some people over others?*

Respect involves showing more concern for people than for agendas, thinking highly of others, building them up in love, and treating everyone with fairness and integrity.

Promise from God   PSALM 112:6, 9   *Those who are righteous will be long remembered. . . . Their good deeds will be remembered forever. They will have influence and honor.*

REST

Why is rest so important?

GENESIS 2:1-3   *The creation of the heavens and the earth and everything in them was completed. On the seventh day God had finished his work of creation, so he rested from all his work. And God blessed the seventh day and declared it holy, because it was the day when he rested from all his work of creation.*

EXODUS 31:17   *[The Sabbath day] is a permanent sign of my covenant with the people of Israel. For in six days the LORD made heaven and earth, but on the seventh day he stopped working and was refreshed.*

Why would the omnipotent God of the universe rest following his work of creation? Surely, it wasn't because the Almighty was physically tired! The answer is that God, in ceasing from his work, called his rest "holy." God knew that you would need to cease from your work to care for your physical and spiritual needs. Work is good, but it must be balanced by regular rest and attention to the health of your soul. Otherwise, you miss the divine moments God sends your way. Make sure to carve out regular times for worship, spiritual refreshment, and rest.

What is the difference between rest and laziness?

PROVERBS 6:10-11 | *A little extra sleep, a little more slumber, a little folding of the hands to rest—then poverty will pounce on you like a bandit; scarcity will attack you like an armed robber.*

MARK 6:31-32 | *Jesus said, "Let's go off by ourselves to a quiet place and rest awhile." He said this because there were so many people coming and going that Jesus and his apostles didn't even have time to eat. So they left by boat for a quiet place, where they could be alone.*

2 THESSALONIANS 3:11 | *Some of you are living idle lives, refusing to work and meddling in other people's business.*

Laziness is always making excuses for why things can't get done. Rest is a reward for a job well done. Someday you will be asked to give an account for how you spent your time here on earth.

Promise from God MATTHEW 11:28 | *Jesus said, "Come to me, all of you who are weary and carry heavy burdens, and I will give you rest."*

RISK

What kinds of risks should Christians take?

GENESIS 12:1 | *The LORD had said to Abram, "Leave your native country, your relatives, and your father's family, and go to the land that I will show you."*

EXODUS 14:1-3, 21-22 | *The LORD gave these instructions to Moses: "Order the Israelites to turn back and camp . . . there along the shore. . . . Then Pharaoh will think, 'The Israelites are confused. They are trapped in the wilderness!'" . . . Then Moses raised his hand over the sea, and the LORD opened up a path through the water with a strong east wind. The wind blew all that night, turning the seabed into dry land. So the people of Israel walked through the middle of the sea on dry ground, with walls of water on each side!*

Abram left everyone and everything he knew to be obedient to God. Moses stood before the Red Sea while Pharaoh's armies, thinking the Israelites were trapped, closed in on them. The waters parted and the people risked the journey through the walls of water to freedom. Great things do not happen without risk. Those great in faith are risk takers.

NUMBERS 14:6-9 | *Two of the men who had explored the land, Joshua son of Nun and Caleb son of Jephunneh, . . . said to all the people of Israel, "The land we traveled through and explored is a wonderful land! And if the LORD is pleased with us, he will bring us safely into that land and give it to us. It is a rich land flowing with milk and honey. Do not rebel against the LORD, and don't be afraid of the people of the land. . . . They have no protection, but the LORD is with us! Don't be afraid of them!"*

Be prepared to risk your resources, your reputation, and possibly even your closest relationships to be faithful to God. Joshua and Caleb, unlike the other spies (see Numbers 13:30-33), were willing to risk all because they trusted God's promises more than the human risks. The only thing more risky than trusting God is *not* trusting him!

LUKE 5:4-7 | *[Jesus] said to Simon, "Now go out where it is deeper, and let down your nets to catch some fish." "Master," Simon replied, "we worked hard all last night and didn't catch a thing. But if you say so, I'll let the nets down again." And this time their nets were so full of fish they began to tear! A shout for help brought their partners in the other boat, and soon both boats were filled with fish and on the verge of sinking.*

Some risks you feel the Lord is asking you to take may appear to be foolish or contrary to your experience. But such risks, done in obedience, yield rich rewards.

ACTS 5:41 | *The apostles left the high council rejoicing that God had counted them worthy to suffer disgrace for the name of Jesus.*

You may risk rejection and loss of security, as the apostles did by preaching about Jesus in the face of persecution, but the rewards of loyalty to God are eternal.

LUKE 5:10-11 | *Jesus replied to Simon, "Don't be afraid! From now on you'll be fishing for people!" And as soon as they landed, they left everything and followed Jesus.*

You may be expected to do difficult things. Risk doing the right thing, even when it is the hardest thing, because it will earn you a reputation for integrity—a priceless quality no one can take from you.

EXODUS 3:10-11 | *[God said,] "Now go, for I am sending you to Pharaoh. You must lead my people Israel out of Egypt." But Moses protested to God, "Who am I to appear before Pharaoh? Who am I to lead the people of Israel out of Egypt?"*

LUKE 1:38 | *Mary responded [to the angel], "I am the Lord's servant. May everything you have said about me come true."*

You must take the risk of doing things God's way. When God asks you to follow him, he often doesn't give you all the information about what will happen. When you step out in faith, he gives guidance as you go. Moses risked his life by approaching Pharaoh and leading the Israelites out of captivity. Mary risked her marriage, her reputation, and her future by being willing to be the mother of Jesus. Following God's will is not without risks, but there is no greater reward.

Promise from God PSALM 37:5 | *Commit everything you do to the LORD. Trust him, and he will help you.*

SAFETY

Does God protect those who love him from physical harm?

PSALM 91:11 | *[The Lord] will order his angels to protect you wherever you go.*

DANIEL 6:22 | *My God sent his angel to shut the lions' mouths so that they would not hurt me.*

Sometimes God protects and delivers you in miraculous ways in order to preserve you so you can continue to serve him.

2 CORINTHIANS 12:7 | *[Paul said,] "I was given a thorn in my flesh, a messenger from Satan to torment me and keep me from becoming proud."*

Sometimes, like Paul, you may experience devastating physical hardship and suffering. These are the times when your faith is put to the test, and you have to keep a perspective that one day all pain and suffering will be gone forever (see Revelation 21:4).

ROMANS 5:3-5 | *We can rejoice, too, when we run into problems and trials, for we know that they help us develop endurance. And endurance develops strength of character, and character strengthens our confident hope of salvation. And this hope will not lead to disappointment. For we know how dearly God loves us, because he has given us the Holy Spirit to fill our hearts with his love.*

When God does not prevent suffering, he promises strength through the Holy Spirit to endure. Enduring suffering may bring you closer to God than being spared from suffering.

If I have an accident, a tragedy, or illness, does it mean God is punishing me for something?

JOHN 9:3 | *"It was not because of his sins or his parents' sins,"* Jesus answered. *"This happened so the power of God could be seen in him."*

God is the redeemer of your suffering and not the cause. Suffering can take you toward God or away from him. If suffering takes you toward God, it is redemptive.

If God doesn't guarantee physical safety, what's the point of faith?

PSALM 23:4 | *Even when I walk through the darkest valley, I will not be afraid, for you are close beside me. Your rod and your staff protect and comfort me.*

JOHN 10:27-29 | *[Jesus said,] "My sheep listen to my voice; I know them, and they follow me. I give them eternal life, and they will never perish. No one can snatch them away from me, for my Father has given them to me, and he is more powerful than anyone else. No one can snatch them from the Father's hand."*

Faith has more to do with the eternal safety of your soul than the physical safety of your body.

2 TIMOTHY 1:12 | *I know the one in whom I trust, and I am sure that he is able to guard what I have entrusted to him until the day of his return.*

Faith is trusting God to guard and keep that which is eternal—your soul.

1 PETER 2:25 | *Once you were like sheep who wandered away. But now you have turned to your Shepherd, the Guardian of your souls.*

Jesus guards your soul from being defeated in spiritual warfare.

1 PETER 3:18 | *Christ suffered for our sins once for all time. He never sinned, but he died for sinners to bring you safely home to God. He suffered physical death, but he was raised to life in the Spirit.*

Faith in Jesus gives you safe passage to your eternal home.

Is it wrong to pray for safety for myself and my loved ones?

ACTS 12:5 | *While Peter was in prison, the church prayed very earnestly for him.*

God always welcomes the expression of your desires when offered in submission to his will.

ROMANS 1:10 | *[Paul said,] "One of the things I always pray for is the opportunity, God willing, to come at last to see you."*

Paul's prayer for safety in travel was rooted in his desire to minister to others.

2 CORINTHIANS 1:11 | *You are helping us by praying for us. Then many people will give thanks because God has graciously answered so many prayers for our safety.*

The early apostles depended on the prayers for safety offered by the churches.

Promise from God PSALM 34:7 | *The angel of the LORD is a guard; he surrounds and defends all who fear him.*

SALVATION

What does it mean to be saved?

ROMANS 3:24 | *God, with undeserved kindness, declares that we are righteous. He did this through Christ Jesus when he freed us from the penalty for our sins.*

ROMANS 4:7-8 | *Oh, what joy for those whose disobedience is forgiven, whose sins are put out of sight. Yes, what joy for those whose record the LORD has cleared of sin.*

Being saved, spiritually speaking, means your sins no longer count against you and you are spared from an eternal death sentence. Instead, they are forgiven by the grace of God, and you are given the free gift of eternal life. Being saved does not spare you from earthly troubles, but it does save you from eternal punishment.

PSALM 51:9-10 | *Remove the stain of my guilt. Create in me a clean heart, O God.*

PSALM 103:12 | *[The Lord] has removed our sins as far from us as the east is from the west.*

Being saved means the stain of guilt has been washed away and you have been completely forgiven by God. Your sins not only *appear* to be gone, they *are* gone! You are given a clean slate!

JOHN 5:24 | *[Jesus said,] "I tell you the truth, those who listen to my message and believe in God who sent me have eternal life. They will never be condemned for their sins, but they have already passed from death into life."*

JOHN 10:27-29 | *[Jesus said,] "My sheep listen to my voice; I know them, and they follow me. I give them eternal life, and they will never perish. No one can snatch them away from me, for my Father has given them to me, and he is more powerful than anyone else. No one can snatch them from the Father's hand."*

Being saved means you are assured of living forever in heaven. You will live on a new earth where there will no longer be sin, pain, or suffering (see Revelation 21:4). What greater hope could you have?

How can I be saved?

ROMANS 10:13 | *Everyone who calls on the name of the LORD will be saved.*

God's Word promises salvation—a guarantee of an eternal, perfect life in heaven—to those who call on Jesus' name to have their sins forgiven. Call out to him in prayer and tell him that you want him to save you. He promises he will.

JOHN 3:16 | *God loved the world so much that he gave his one and only Son, so that everyone who believes in him will not perish but have eternal life.*

ROMANS 3:20-22 | *No one can ever be made right with God by doing what the law commands. The law simply shows us how sinful we are. But now God has shown us a way to be made right with him without keeping the requirements of the law, as was promised in the writings of Moses and the prophets long ago. We are made right with God by placing our faith in Jesus Christ. And this is true for everyone who believes, no matter who we are.*

Jesus promises that those who believe in him will be saved. All you have to do is accept what Jesus did for you. God sent Jesus Christ to take your place and to receive the punishment that your sins demanded. When you believe that he died to save you from your sins and rose again to give you eternal life, then you are saved.

ROMANS 10:9-10 | *If you confess with your mouth that Jesus is Lord and believe in your heart that God raised him from the dead, you will be saved. For it is by believing in your heart that you are made right with God, and it is by confessing with your mouth that you are saved.*

EPHESIANS 2:8 | *God saved you by his grace when you believed. And you can't take credit for this; it is a gift from God.*

It seems too easy. The greatest gift God could ever offer—life in a perfect world—is absolutely free. You just have to accept it by (1) agreeing with God that you have sinned, (2) acknowledging that your sin cuts you off from God, (3) asking Jesus to forgive your sins, and (4) believing that Jesus is Lord over everything and that he is the Son of God. The gift is yours.

ROMANS 11:6 | *It is not by their good works. For in that case, God's grace would not be what it really is—free and undeserved.*

You cannot earn your way to heaven by being good and doing kind deeds. Salvation comes only through faith in Jesus.

Is salvation available to anyone?

LUKE 2:11-12 | *The Savior—yes, the Messiah, the Lord—has been born today in Bethlehem . . . ! And you will recognize him by this sign: You will find a baby wrapped snugly in strips of cloth, lying in a manger.*

Jesus was born in a humble stable among very ordinary people to powerfully demonstrate that salvation is available to anyone who sincerely seeks him.

HEBREWS 9:27 | *Each person is destined to die once and after that comes judgment.*

REVELATION 20:12 | *I saw the dead, both great and small, standing before God's throne. And the books were opened, including the Book of Life. And the dead were judged according to what they had done.*

Salvation is available to all, but a time will come when it will be too late to receive it.

How can I be sure of my salvation?

ROMANS 10:9 | *If you confess with your mouth that Jesus is Lord and believe in your heart that God raised him from the dead, you will be saved.*

You can be sure of your salvation because God has promised that you are saved if you believe in Jesus Christ as your Savior.

JOHN 1:12 | *To all who believed him and accepted him, he gave the right to become children of God.*

Just as a child cannot be "un-born," God's children—those who have believed in Jesus Christ—cannot be "un-born-again."

Why is salvation so central to Christianity?

ROMANS 3:23 | *Everyone has sinned; we all fall short of God's glorious standard.*

ROMANS 6:23 | *The wages of sin is death.*

COLOSSIANS 1:22 | *[God] has reconciled you to himself through the death of Christ in his physical body. As a result, he has brought you into his own presence, and you are holy and blameless as you stand before him without a single fault.*

1 THESSALONIANS 3:13 | *May [the Lord] . . . make your hearts strong, blameless, and holy as you stand before God our Father when our Lord Jesus comes again with all his holy people.*

Salvation is necessary because sin against a holy God separates you from him, bringing judgment and spiritual death. An unholy being cannot live in the presence of a holy God.

ACTS 4:12 | *There is salvation in no one else! God has given no other name under heaven by which we must be saved.*

Although it may sound exclusive, the Bible's claim of "one way" to salvation is actually an expression of the grace and kindness of God in letting all people know how to escape eternal judgment. God invites anyone and everyone to come to him.

Promise from God ROMANS 10:9 | *If you confess with your mouth that Jesus is Lord and believe in your heart that God raised him from the dead, you will be saved.*

SATISFACTION

Why do so many people seem so unhappy?

PSALM 63:1, 5 | *O God, you are my God; I earnestly search for you. My soul thirsts for you; my whole body longs for you in this parched and weary land where there is no water. . . . You satisfy me more than the richest feast.*

ECCLESIASTES 1:8 | *No matter how much we see, we are never satisfied. No matter how much we hear, we are not content.*

ISAIAH 55:2 | *Listen to me, and you will eat what is good. You will enjoy the finest food.*

JOHN 4:14 | *Those who drink the water I give will never be thirsty again. It becomes a fresh, bubbling spring within them, giving them eternal life.*

Too many people try to meet their deepest needs in ways that just don't satisfy. Sometimes when you're hungry, the worst thing you can do is eat the wrong thing. For example, if you haven't eaten in a while and you quickly gobble down three doughnuts, you'll be satisfied for a few minutes—until you start to shake from the sugar rush. The same principle applies to satisfying the hungry soul. If you fill it with fun and pleasure and sin, you'll always be craving more but not getting enough. Your soul will get the "shakes." Without taking nourishment from God's spiritual food, you will never feel satisfied and you'll wonder what is wrong with your life.

Does God promise to satisfy all my needs?

PROVERBS 30:8 | *Give me just enough to satisfy my needs.*

God's first task is often to redefine your needs. There is a vast difference between your needs and your wants. Don't confuse the two.

PSALM 17:15 | *When I awake, I will see you face to face and be satisfied.*

Spiritual need finds satisfaction in intimacy with God. Since he created you for this purpose, the only way you'll be satisfied is to pursue a relationship with him.

MATTHEW 5:3 | *[Jesus said,] "God blesses those who . . . realize their need for him, for the Kingdom of Heaven is theirs."*

Jesus promised that the heart hungry for righteousness will be satisfied. Be sure you are hungry for the food that truly satisfies.

Promise from God PSALM 107:9 | *[The Lord] satisfies the thirsty and fills the hungry with good things.*

SELF-CONTROL

Why can't I seem to control certain desires?

ROMANS 7:21-25 | *I have discovered this principle of life—that when I want to do what is right, I inevitably do what is wrong. I love God's law with all my heart. But there is another power within me that is at war with my mind. This power makes me a slave to the sin that is still within me. Oh, what a miserable person I am! Who will free me from this life that is dominated by sin and death? Thank God! The answer is in Jesus Christ our Lord. So you see how it is: In my mind I really want to obey God's law, but because of my sinful nature I am a slave to sin.*

Because you were born with a sinful nature, it will always be a struggle for you to do what is right and to not do what is wrong. Thankfully, God understands your weaknesses and gives you the desire to please him. As you obey God, you will develop more self-control and the battle with your sinful nature will lessen.

ROMANS 12:1 | *Give your bodies to God because of all he has done for you. Let them be a living and holy sacrifice—the kind he will find acceptable. This is truly the way to worship him.*

You must truly want to give up the wrong desires you have.

What are some steps to exercising self-control?

PSALM 119:9 | *How can a . . . person stay pure? By obeying your word.*

2 TIMOTHY 2:5 | *Athletes cannot win the prize unless they follow the rules.*

To develop self-control, you first need to know God's guidelines for right living as found in the Bible. You need to know what you must control before you can keep it under control. Reading God's Word consistently—preferably every day—keeps his guidelines for right living fresh in your mind.

1 TIMOTHY 4:8 | *Physical training is good, but training for godliness is much better, promising benefits in this life and in the life to come.*

Self-control begins with God's work in you, but it requires your effort as well. Just as talented musicians and athletes must develop their talent, strength, and coordination through intentional effort, spiritual fitness must be intentional as well. God promises to reward such effort.

1 CORINTHIANS 10:13 | *The temptations in your life are no different from what others experience. And God is faithful. He will not allow the temptation to be more than you can stand. When you are tempted, he will show you a way out so that you can endure.*

You're not alone in your trials and temptations. Instead of thinking you have no hope for resisting, call on the Lord to lead you out of temptation. Ask trusted friends to keep you accountable. If you ask, God promises to give you what you need in order to resist.

PSALM 141:3 | *Take control of what I say, O LORD, and guard my lips.*

PROVERBS 13:3 | *Those who control their tongue will have a long life; opening your mouth can ruin everything.*

JAMES 1:26 | *If you claim to be religious but don't control your tongue, you are fooling yourself, and your religion is worthless.*

You exercise self-control by being careful of what you say. How often do you wish you could take back words as soon as they have left your mouth?

ROMANS 8:6 | *Letting your sinful nature control your mind leads to death. But letting the Spirit control your mind leads to life and peace.*

In order to have self-control, you must let God take control of your mind by fighting against the desires you know are wrong.

Promise from God JAMES 1:12 | *God blesses those who patiently endure testing and temptation. Afterward they will receive the crown of life that God has promised to those who love him.*

SELFISHNESS

Why is selfishness so destructive?

GENESIS 13:8-11 | *Abram said to Lot, "Let's not allow this conflict to come between us or our herdsmen. After all, we are close relatives! The whole countryside is open to you. Take your choice of any section of the land you want, and we will separate." . . . Lot* *took a long look at the fertile plains of the Jordan Valley. . . . The whole area was well watered everywhere, like the garden of the LORD. . . . Lot chose for himself the whole Jordan Valley.*

GENESIS 27:35-37, 41 | *Isaac said, "Your brother was here, and he tricked me. He has taken away your blessing." Esau exclaimed, "No wonder his name is Jacob, for now he has cheated me twice. First he took my rights as the firstborn, and now he has stolen my blessing. Oh, haven't you saved even one blessing for me?" Isaac said to Esau, "I have made Jacob your master and have declared that all his brothers will be his servants." . . . From that time on, Esau hated Jacob. . . . And Esau began to scheme: . . . "I will kill my brother."*

Selfishness can destroy relationships and tear families apart. *Selflessness* can strengthen relationships and bring families closer together. Abram recognized that and sacrificed personal gain for the sake of his family, while Esau and Jacob struggled with selfishness.

ACTS 8:18 | *When Simon saw that the Spirit was given when the apostles laid their hands on people, he offered them money to buy this power.*

Selfish ambition can cause you to do almost anything for personal gain.

How can I address the selfishness in my own life?

MARK 8:34 | *Calling the crowd to join his disciples, [Jesus] said, "If any of you wants to be my follower, you must turn from your selfish ways, take up your cross, and follow me."*

GALATIANS 2:20 | *My old self has been crucified with Christ. It is no longer I who live, but Christ lives in me. So I live in this earthly body by trusting in the Son of God, who loved me and gave himself for me.*

When you surrender to God, you give up what you think is best for your life and do what he knows is best. You put aside your self-promoting ambitions so that you can do the job Jesus has for you. You ask Jesus, through the power of the Holy Spirit, to live in you and through you.

MATTHEW 20:28 | *Even the Son of Man came not to be served but to serve others and to give his life as a ransom for many.*

1 CORINTHIANS 10:24 | *Don't be concerned for your own good but for the good of others.*

PHILIPPIANS 2:3 | *Don't be selfish; don't try to impress others. Be humble, thinking of others as better than yourselves.*

JAMES 3:16 | *Wherever there is jealousy and selfish ambition, there you will find disorder and evil of every kind.*

Selfish motives produce selfish actions. To escape selfishness, you have to truly want what is best for others more than what you desire for yourself.

1 JOHN 3:17 | *If someone has enough money to live well and sees a brother or sister in need but shows no compassion—how can God's love be in that person?*

One of the best cures for a selfish heart is generous giving.

It's a dog-eat-dog world out there. If I don't look out for myself, who will?

LUKE 14:8, 10-11 | *When you are invited to a wedding feast, don't sit in the seat of honor. . . . Instead, take the lowest place at the foot of the table. Then when your host sees you, he will come* and say, *"Friend, we have a better place for you!" Then you will be honored in front of all the other guests. For those who exalt themselves will be humbled, and those who humble themselves will be exalted.*

The highest honor from God awaits those who live their lives trying to serve and honor others.

PHILIPPIANS 4:19 | *This same God who takes care of me will supply all your needs from his glorious riches, which have been given to us in Christ Jesus.*

When you allow Jesus to take charge of your life, you can be assured that he is watching out for you, and thus you are freed from worrying about your own needs and able to focus on others.

Promise from God MATTHEW 16:25 | *[Jesus said,] "If you try to hang on to your life, you will lose it. But if you give up your life for my sake, you will save it."*

SERVICE

The whole idea of service seems to run counter to what I was taught—to do my own thing. What does it mean to be a servant?

PHILIPPIANS 2:6-8 | *Though he was God, [Christ Jesus] did not think of equality with God as something to cling to. Instead, he gave up his divine privileges. . . . He humbled himself in obedience to God.*

A servant is humble and obedient to God.

MATTHEW 20:26-28 | *Whoever wants to be a leader among you must be your servant, and whoever wants to be first among you must become your slave. For even the Son of Man came not to be served but to serve others and to give his life as a ransom for many.*

A servant ministers to others regardless of their status in life.

JOHN 13:5 | *[Jesus] began to wash the disciples' feet, drying them with the towel he had around him.*

A servant gladly performs tasks that others consider beneath them.

ROMANS 6:13 | *Give yourselves completely to God. . . . Use your whole body as an instrument to do what is right for the glory of God.*

A servant uses all his or her energy and talents for the benefit of God and others.

What are some requirements to serve God?

PSALM 2:11 | *Serve the LORD with reverent fear, and rejoice with trembling.*

A joyful heart and reverent awe of God.

PSALM 42:1-2 | *As the deer longs for streams of water, so I long for you, O God. I thirst for God, the living God.*

PSALM 119:59 | *I pondered the direction of my life, and I turned to follow your laws.*

A desire to please God and walk in his ways.

MATTHEW 6:24 | *No one can serve two masters. For you will hate one and love the other; you will be devoted to one and despise the other.*

Loyalty to God.

ROMANS 7:6 | *Now we can serve God, not in the old way of obeying the letter of the law, but in the new way of living in the Spirit.*

A desire to be led by the Holy Spirit.

ACTS 20:19 | *I have done the Lord's work humbly and with many tears. I have endured the trials that came to me.*

Humility.

GALATIANS 5:13 | *You have been called to live in freedom, my brothers and sisters. But don't use your freedom to satisfy your sinful nature. Instead, use your freedom to serve one another in love.*

Love for others.

How can I serve God today?

JOSHUA 22:5 | *Be very careful to obey all the commands and the instructions that Moses gave to you. Love the LORD your God, walk in all his ways, obey his commands, hold firmly to him, and serve him with all your heart and all your soul.*

Obey God's Word, which will motivate you to want to help others even when it's not convenient.

JOSHUA 24:14-15 | *Fear the LORD and serve him wholeheartedly. . . . Choose today whom you will serve. . . . As for me and my family, we will serve the LORD.*

Honor God by making your relationship with him your first priority; then you will want to do what he asks.

1 CORINTHIANS 12:5 | *There are different kinds of service, but we serve the same Lord.*

Exercise your spiritual gifts. Serve the Lord by discovering your spiritual gifts and enthusiastically investing them in the ministry of the church (see Romans 12:6-8; 1 Corinthians 12:4-11; 1 Peter 4:10-11).

MATTHEW 25:23 | *You have been faithful in handling this small amount, so now I will give you many more responsibilities.*

Demonstrate love and kindness to all people, especially those in need. Regardless of the level of your gifts and abilities, God expects you to invest what he's given you into the lives of others.

ROMANS 12:11 | *Never be lazy, but work hard and serve the Lord enthusiastically.*

Serve with enthusiasm and your attitude will not only energize you, it will also rub off on others.

Promise from God JOHN 15:10-12 | *[Jesus said,] "When you obey my commandments, you remain in my love. . . . I have told you these things so that you will be filled with my joy. Yes, your joy will overflow! This is my commandment: Love each other in the same way I have loved you."*

SEX

What does God think about sex?

GENESIS 1:27-28 | *God created human beings in his own image . . . male and female he created them. Then God blessed them and said, "Be fruitful and multiply."*

GENESIS 2:24 | *A man leaves his father and mother and is joined to his wife, and the two are united into one.*

God created sex. He made man and woman sexual beings, with the ability to express love to and delight in each other and to reproduce and replenish the next generations. The sexual relationship is a key part of a husband and wife's becoming one person. God intended sex to be a good thing within the context of the marriage relationship.

PROVERBS 5:18-19 | *Let your wife be a fountain of blessing for you. Rejoice in the wife of your youth. . . . Let her breasts satisfy you always. May you always be captivated by her love.*

SONG OF SONGS 7:6 | *Oh, how beautiful you are! How pleasing, my love, how full of delights!*

God clearly allows delight in sex within marriage. Sex is not for reproduction only, but also for a bonding of love and enjoyment between husband and wife.

SONG OF SONGS 7:11 | *Come, my love, let us go out to the fields and spend the night among the wildflowers.*

When marriage becomes routine, it is important to rekindle the fires of sexual intimacy.

Is it so bad if I just think about sex with someone other than my spouse? I don't really do anything.

EXODUS 20:17 | *You must not covet your neighbor's house. You must not covet your neighbor's wife.*

MATTHEW 5:27-28 | *[Jesus said,] "You have heard the commandment that says, 'You must not commit adultery.' But I say, anyone who even looks at a woman with lust has already committed adultery with her in his heart."*

Lust is adultery in the heart. While it is true that when you only imagine having sex with someone you have not consummated the act, it is also true that according to Jesus' words you have committed adultery.

MARK 7:20-22 | *It is what comes from inside that defiles you. For from within, out of a person's heart, come evil thoughts, sexual immorality, . . . lustful desires.*

What you think about doesn't come just from your mind; it comes from your heart as well. Your thoughts tell you the condition of your heart, and your every action begins as a thought. Left unchecked, wrong thoughts will eventually result in wrong actions. If you continue to think about having sex with someone other than your spouse, your heart will begin to convince your mind that what you want to do is okay. The Bible says that the heart is "desperately wicked" (Jeremiah 17:9). In other words, don't trust your thoughts and emotions to tell you what is right and good. Trust God's Word, for it comes from God's heart, which is good and perfect.

Promise from God 1 CORINTHIANS 10:13 | *The temptations in your life are no different from what others experience. And God is faithful. He will not allow the temptation to be more than you can stand. When you are tempted, he will show you a way out so that you can endure.*

SINGLENESS

Is God's plan for everyone to marry? If I'm single, am I missing out on God's plan for me?

MATTHEW 19:12 | *Some choose not to marry for the sake of the Kingdom of Heaven.*

1 CORINTHIANS 7:7 | *Each person has a special gift from God, of one kind or another.*

Either marriage or singleness can be a gift from God. Is it all right to remain single? Yes. Is it all right to marry? Yes. There are advantages to both.

1 CORINTHIANS 7:32 | *An unmarried man can spend his time doing the Lord's work and thinking how to please him.*

In your singleness, serve the Lord wholeheartedly. Do not give in to the feeling that your life is incomplete without a spouse.

What if I want to marry? Is that wrong?

GENESIS 2:18 | *The LORD God said, "It is not good for the man to be alone. I will make a helper who is just right for him."*

1 CORINTHIANS 7:38 | *The person who marries his fiancée does well, and the person who doesn't marry does even better.*

God made man and woman for each other. It is good when the right mates find each other, but it's tragic when a marriage falls short of God's glorious plan. People should not feel pressured either to marry or to remain single. Ask God to lead you concerning marriage and the right marriage partner.

How can God help me accept my singleness?

1 CORINTHIANS 7:7-8 | *[Paul said,] "I wish everyone were single, just as I am. Yet each person has a special gift from God, of one kind or another. So I say to those who aren't married and to widows—it's better to stay unmarried, just as I am."*

1 CORINTHIANS 7:17 | *Each of you should continue to live in whatever situation the Lord has placed you.*

Sometimes, when you desperately want something, it is easy to forget the gifts of your current situation. Paul found that his singleness was an advantage in pursuing his call of establishing churches. Step back and look for how God might want to use you in your singleness in a way that he could not if you were married.

If a person's mate has died, is it all right to marry again?

1 CORINTHIANS 7:39 | *A wife is bound to her husband as long as he lives. If her husband dies, she is free to marry anyone she wishes, but only if he loves the Lord.*

Marriage is a lifetime commitment. When a mate dies, the marriage contract is over. It is not wrong for the survivor to marry again.

Promise from God PHILIPPIANS 4:19 | *God . . . will supply all your needs from his glorious riches, which have been given to us in Christ Jesus.*

SPIRITUAL WARFARE

What does the Bible say about spiritual warfare?

EPHESIANS 6:11-12 | *Put on all of God's armor so that you will be able to stand firm against all strategies of the devil. For we are not fighting against flesh-and-blood enemies, but against evil rulers and authorities of the unseen world, against mighty powers in this dark world, and against evil spirits in the heavenly places.*

Spiritual warfare is the unseen battle that is being waged for your soul. Winning this battle requires preparation—through prayer, unwavering faith, and knowledge of biblical truth—to defeat your spiritual enemy.

1 PETER 5:8 | *Stay alert! Watch out for your great enemy, the devil. He prowls around like a roaring lion, looking for someone to devour.*

You must be alert at all times for the sneak attacks of the devil.

PHILIPPIANS 2:10 | *At the name of Jesus every knee should bow, in heaven and on earth and under the earth.*

JAMES 4:7 | *Resist the devil, and he will flee from you.*

When you resist the devil in the name and power of Jesus, he will flee from you. At the name of Jesus, Satan has no power.

MATTHEW 4:1, 3-4 | *Jesus was led by the Spirit into the wilderness to be tempted there by the devil. . . . During that time the devil came and said to him, "If you are the Son of God, tell these stones to become loaves of bread." But Jesus told him, "No! The Scriptures say . . ."*

When under attack by Satan, Jesus relied on the Word of God to combat the lies of his adversary.

Promise from God EPHESIANS 6:11 | *Put on all of God's armor so that you will be able to stand firm against all strategies of the devil.*

STRESS

What are some of the dangers of stress?

NUMBERS 11:10-11, 13-15 | *Moses was . . . very aggravated. And Moses said to the LORD, "Why are you treating me, your servant, so harshly? . . . What did I do to deserve the burden of all these people? . . . Where am I supposed to get meat for all these people? They keep whining to me, saying, 'Give us meat to eat!' I can't carry all these people by myself! The load is far too heavy! If this is how you intend to treat me, just go ahead and kill me. Do me a favor and spare me this misery!"*

2 CORINTHIANS 1:8 | *We think you ought to know, dear brothers and sisters, about the trouble we went through in the province of Asia. We were crushed and overwhelmed beyond our ability to endure, and we thought we would never live through it.*

The intense demands of life have the potential to overwhelm you. The expectations, the criticism, the scope of the need and responsibility are threats to even the strongest person.

MATTHEW 13:22 | *The seed that fell among the thorns represents those who hear God's word, but all too quickly the message is crowded out by the worries of this life.*

LUKE 10:40-41 | *Martha was distracted by the big dinner she was preparing. She came to Jesus and said, "Lord, doesn't it seem unfair to you that my sister just sits here while I do all the work? Tell her to come and help me." But the Lord said to her, "My dear Martha, you are worried and upset over all these details!"*

Stress can cause you to focus on the trivial and miss the important. As pressure squeezes your perspective inward, you lose the big picture. Preoccupation with the issues of the moment blinds you to what's really important.

How can I deal with stress?

2 CORINTHIANS 4:9 | *We are hunted down, but never abandoned by God. We get knocked down, but we are not destroyed.*

Keep going! Knowing that God is by your side during times of trouble and stress can help you to not give up.

PSALM 55:22 | *Give your burdens to the LORD, and he will take care of you.*

MATTHEW 11:28 | *Jesus said, "Come to me, all of you who are weary and carry heavy burdens, and I will give you rest."*

Bring your burdens to the Lord. Only he brings true peace of heart and mind. God's availability and promises provide effective stress reducers.

2 SAMUEL 22:7 | *In my distress I cried out to the LORD. . . . He heard me from his sanctuary; my cry reached his ears.*

PSALM 86:7 | *I will call to you whenever I'm in trouble, and you will answer me.*

Be persistent in prayer.

MARK 6:31 | *Jesus said, "Let's go off by ourselves to a quiet place and rest awhile." He said this because there were so many people coming and going that Jesus and his apostles didn't even have time to eat.*

Take time to slow down and take a break from pressure-packed situations.

1 CORINTHIANS 6:19-20 | *Don't you realize that your body is the temple of the Holy Spirit, who lives in you and was given to you by God? You do not belong to yourself, for God bought you with a high price. So you must honor God with your body.*

Take care of your body. Adequate rest, regular exercise, and proper nutrition are essential to dealing effectively with stress.

GALATIANS 6:9 | *Let's not get tired of doing what is good. At just the right time we will reap a harvest of blessing if we don't give up.*

Don't let stress defeat you. When you are tired of doing good, you may be just too tired.

ISAIAH 41:10 | *Don't be afraid, for I am with you. Don't be discouraged, for I am your God. I will strengthen you and help you. I will hold you up with my victorious right hand.*

Turn from fear and anxiety to faith and peace. God promises to supply the power to get you through the hard times.

Promise from God JOHN 16:33 | *I have told you all this so that you may have peace in me. Here on earth you will have many trials and sorrows. But take heart, because I have overcome the world.*

SUCCESS

What is true success in God's eyes?

MATTHEW 22:37 | *Jesus [said], "You must love the LORD your God with all your heart, all your soul, and all your mind."*

JOHN 15:8 | *[Jesus said,] "When you produce much fruit, you are my true disciples. This brings great glory to my Father."*

Success is knowing God and living in a way that will be pleasing to him.

ACTS 16:31 | *Believe in the Lord Jesus and you will be saved.*

JOHN 17:3 | *This is the way to have eternal life—to know you, the only true God, and Jesus Christ, the one you sent to earth.*

Faith in Jesus is success because only through faith will you find salvation and eternal life.

JOSHUA 1:8-9 | *Study this Book of Instruction continually. Meditate on it day and night so you will be sure to obey everything written in it. Only then will you prosper and succeed in all you do. . . . For the LORD your God is with you wherever you go.*

PSALM 25:4-5 | *Show me the right path, O LORD; point out the road for me to follow. Lead me by your truth and teach me.*

Studying the Bible reveals God's will for your life, which is the most successful path you can take.

MATTHEW 20:25-26 | *Rulers in this world lord it over their people, and officials flaunt their authority over those under them. But among you it will be different. Whoever wants to be a leader among you must be your servant.*

Serving and helping others brings success, for in serving others you find true joy.

JOHN 15:8, 16 | *When you produce much fruit, you are my true disciples. This brings great glory to my Father. . . . You didn't choose me. I chose you. I appointed you to go and produce lasting fruit, so that the Father will give you whatever you ask for, using my name.*

Success is being productive—producing results that matter to God.

PROVERBS 16:3 | *Commit your actions to the LORD, and your plans will succeed.*

Committing all you do to God is success. Put God first in your life, for only then can you fully understand what is really important in life.

Promise from God PSALM 60:12 | *With God's help we will do mighty things.*

SUFFERING

Why am I suffering? Doesn't God care about me?

GENESIS 37:28 | *When the Ishmaelites, who were Midianite traders, came by, Joseph's brothers pulled him out of the cistern and sold him to them for twenty pieces of silver. And the traders took him to Egypt.*

JEREMIAH 32:18 | *You show unfailing love to thousands, but you also bring the consequences of one generation's sin upon the next.*

Sometimes you suffer because of the sins of others, not your own sins.

JOB 1:19 | *The house collapsed, and all your children are dead.*

JOHN 9:2-3 | *"Rabbi," his disciples asked him, "why was this man born blind? Was it because of his own sins or his parents' sins?" "It was not because of his sins or his parents' sins," Jesus answered. "This happened so the power of God could be seen in him."*

Sometimes the suffering that comes to you just happens, for no reason you can see. It is how you react to the suffering that matters.

GENESIS 3:6, 23 | *[The woman] saw that the tree was beautiful and its fruit looked delicious. . . . So she took some of the fruit and ate it. Then she gave some to her husband, who was with her, and he ate it, too. . . . So the LORD God banished them from the Garden of Eden.*

PROVERBS 3:11-12 | *My child, don't reject the LORD's discipline, and don't be upset when he corrects you. For the LORD corrects those he loves, just as a father corrects a child in whom he delights.*

Sometimes God sends suffering as punishment for sin. He may discipline you because he loves you and wants to correct you and restore you to him. Thank God for this kind of suffering because his actions to get your attention could save you from even greater consequences later.

DEUTERONOMY 8:2 | *Remember how the LORD your God led you through the wilderness for these forty years, humbling you and testing you to prove your character, and to find out whether or not you would obey his commands.*

Sometimes God tests you with suffering to encourage you to obey him.

1 PETER 4:14 | *Be happy when you are insulted for being a Christian, for then the glorious Spirit of God rests upon you.*

Sometimes your suffering comes because you have taken a stand for Jesus.

JAMES 1:3 | *When your faith is tested, your endurance has a chance to grow.*

Sometimes your suffering is designed to help you grow and mature.

2 CORINTHIANS 1:3-4 | *God is our merciful Father and the source of all comfort. He comforts us in all our troubles so that we can comfort others. When they are troubled, we will be able to give them the same comfort God has given us.*

Suffering enables you to comfort others. Wounded healers are more effective than healers who have never been wounded—those who have scars can truly empathize with others who are hurting. Being wounded may appear to weaken you, but actually it makes you stronger.

Can any good come from suffering?

JOB 5:17-18 | *Consider the joy of those corrected by God! Do not despise the discipline of the Almighty when you sin. For though he wounds, he also bandages. He strikes, but his hands also heal.*

Suffering brings great renewal and healing if it drives you to God.

2 CORINTHIANS 12:10 | *That's why I take pleasure in my weaknesses, and in the insults, hardships, persecutions, and troubles that I suffer for Christ. For when I am weak, then I am strong.*

Suffering is *good* when you learn from your mistakes so you avoid repeating them in the future or when you grow stronger from an unfortunate experience.

PROVERBS 10:25 | *When the storms of life come, the wicked are whirled away, but the godly have a lasting foundation.*

ISAIAH 33:2 | *LORD, be merciful to us, for we have waited for you. Be our strong arm each day and our salvation in times of trouble.*

The great message of the Bible is that God promises to bring renewal, healing, and spiritual maturity through your suffering so that you are stronger and better equipped to help others and to live with purpose and meaning.

2 TIMOTHY 2:10 | *I am willing to endure anything if it will bring salvation and eternal glory in Christ Jesus to those God has chosen.*

When suffering is for your good, for Christ's glory, and for the building up of his church, you should be glad to accept it.

How do I stay close to God in times of suffering?

PSALM 22:24 | *[The LORD] has not ignored or belittled the suffering of the needy. He has not turned his back on them, but has listened to their cries for help.*

Recognize that God has not abandoned you.

LAMENTATIONS 3:32-33 | *Though [the LORD] brings grief, he also shows compassion because of the greatness of his unfailing love. For he does not enjoy hurting people or causing them sorrow.*

Recognize that God does not want to see you suffer. A loving God does not enjoy the suffering that comes your way. But his compassionate love and care will see you through your times of pain.

LUKE 24:26 | *Wasn't it clearly predicted that the Messiah would have to suffer all these things before entering his glory?*

COLOSSIANS 1:24 | *I am glad when I suffer for you in my body, for I am participating in the sufferings of Christ that continue for his body, the church.*

Recognize that Jesus himself suffered for you. He suffered the agonies of the Cross, which was incredible physical suffering, but he also bore the unthinkable weight of the sins of the world.

ROMANS 8:17-18 | *Since we are his children, we are his heirs. In fact, together with Christ we are heirs of God's glory. But if we are to share his glory, we must also share his suffering. Yet what we suffer now is nothing compared to the glory he will reveal to us later.*

HEBREWS 2:18 | *Since [Jesus] himself has gone through suffering and testing, he is able to help us when we are being tested.*

Recognize that suffering is not forever and will end when those who believe in Jesus are welcomed into heaven.

Promise from God PSALM 147:3 | *He heals the brokenhearted and bandages their wounds.*

TEMPTATION

Is temptation sin?

MATTHEW 4:1 | *Jesus was led by the Spirit into the wilderness to be tempted there by the devil.*

HEBREWS 4:14-15 | *Jesus . . . faced all of the same testings we do, yet he did not sin.*

Jesus was severely tempted, yet he never gave in to temptation. Since Jesus was tempted and remained sinless, we know that being tempted is not the same as sinning. You don't have to feel guilty about the temptations you wrestle with. Rather, you can devote yourself to resisting them.

Does my temptation ever come from God?

JAMES 1:13 | *When you are being tempted, do not say, "God is tempting me." God is never tempted to do wrong, and he never tempts anyone else.*

Temptation originates not in the mind of God but in the mind of Satan, who plants it in your heart. Victory over temptation originates in the mind of God and flows to your heart.

JAMES 1:2 | *When troubles come your way, consider it an opportunity for great joy.*

Although God does not send temptation, he brings good from it by helping you grow stronger through it.

Why is temptation so enticing to me?

GENESIS 3:6 | *[The woman] saw that the tree was beautiful and its fruit looked delicious. . . . So she took some of the fruit and ate it.*

Satan's favorite strategy is to make that which is sinful appear to be desirable and good. In contrast, he also tries to make good look evil. If Satan can make evil look good and good look evil, then your giving in to temptation appears right instead of wrong. You must constantly be aware of the confusion he desires to create in you.

1 KINGS 11:1-3 | *Solomon loved many foreign women. . . . The LORD had clearly instructed the people of Israel, "You must not marry them, because they will turn your hearts to their gods." . . . And in fact, they did turn his heart away from the LORD.*

Often, temptation begins in seemingly harmless pleasure, soon gets out of control, and progresses to full-blown idolatry. But the reality is that the kind of pleasure that leads to sin is never harmless. Before you give in to something that seems innocent, take a look at God's Word to see what it says. If Solomon had done this, he would have been reminded that his "pleasure" was really sin. Maybe he would have been convicted enough to stop.

How can I resist temptation?

1 TIMOTHY 4:7-8 | *Do not waste time. . . . Train yourself to be godly. "Physical training is good, but training for godliness is much better, promising benefits in this life and in the life to come."*

To overcome temptation, you need to prepare for it before it presses in on you. Train yourself in the quieter times so that you will have the spiritual wisdom, strength, and commitment to honor God in the face of intense desires and temptation.

GENESIS 39:12 | *She came and grabbed him by his cloak, demanding, "Come on, sleep with me!" Joseph tore himself away . . . [and] ran from the house.*

If possible, remove yourself from the tempting situation. Sometimes you must literally flee.

MATTHEW 6:9, 13 | *Pray like this: . . . Don't let us yield to temptation, but rescue us from the evil one.*

Make resisting temptation a constant focus of prayer.

ECCLESIASTES 4:12 | *A person standing alone can be attacked and defeated, but two can stand back-to-back and conquer. Three are even better, for a triple-braided cord is not easily broken.*

Enlisting a Christian friend as an accountability partner will give you far more spiritual strength than you have on your own.

1 JOHN 5:21 | *Keep away from anything that might take God's place in your hearts.*

Avoid tempting situations and people.

JAMES 4:7 | *Resist the devil, and he will flee from you.*

1 PETER 5:8-9 | *Stay alert! Watch out for your great enemy, the devil. He prowls around like a roaring lion, looking for someone to devour. Stand firm against him, and be strong in your faith.*

The devil has less power than you think. He can tempt you, but he cannot coerce you. He can dangle the bait in front of you, but he cannot force you to take it. You can resist the devil as Jesus did: by responding to the lies of the tempter with the truth of God's Word (see Matthew 4:1-11).

Promise from God   1 CORINTHIANS 10:13 | *The temptations in your life are no different from what others experience. And God is faithful. He will not allow the temptation to be more than you can stand. When you are tempted, he will show you a way out so that you can endure.*

TESTING

How is testing different from temptation?

1 PETER 1:7 | *These trials will show that your faith is genuine. It is being tested as fire tests and purifies gold—though your faith is far more precious than mere gold.*

Where Satan tempts to destroy your faith, God tests to strengthen and purify it.

JAMES 1:3 | *When your faith is tested, your endurance has a chance to grow.*

Temptations try to make you quit. Testing tries to help you endure and not quit.

What good comes out of being tested?

GENESIS 22:1 | *God tested Abraham's faith.*

Out of testing comes a more committed faith. Just as commercial products are tested to strengthen their performance, so also God tests your faith to strengthen your resolve so you can accomplish all God wants you to.

JEREMIAH 6:27 | *[The Lord said,] "Jeremiah, I have made you a tester of metals, that you may determine the quality of my people."*

Spiritual testing reveals the impurities in your heart. Once you are able to recognize your sins and shortcomings, you can let God forgive and remove them, making you stronger and more pure.

DEUTERONOMY 13:3 | *The LORD your God is testing you to see if you truly love him with all your heart and soul.*

God's testing results in a deepening of your obedience and love for him.

DEUTERONOMY 8:2 | *Remember how the LORD your God led you through the wilderness for these forty years, humbling you and testing you to prove your character.*

Testing develops maturity of character. Character is strengthened not through ease but through adversity.

JAMES 1:2-4 | *When troubles come your way, consider it an opportunity for great joy. For you know that when your faith is tested, your endurance has a chance to grow. So let it grow, for when your endurance is fully developed, you will be perfect and complete, needing nothing.*

Testing develops endurance. It trains you to persist to the end rather than give up before you get there.

LUKE 8:13 | *The seeds on the rocky soil represent those who hear the message and receive it with joy. But since they don't have deep roots, they believe for a while, then they fall away when they face temptation.*

Testing reveals the strength of your commitment.

Promise from God JAMES 1:12 | *God blesses those who patiently endure testing and temptation. Afterward they will receive the crown of life that God has promised to those who love him.*

THANKFULNESS

Why should I give thanks to God?

1 CHRONICLES 16:34 | *Give thanks to the LORD, for he is good! His faithful love endures forever.*

Give thanks to God because he is always good and because he will always love you no matter what you've done. Thanking God for his character helps you more fully appreciate and respect the qualities in him and in others.

LUKE 17:16 | *He fell to the ground at Jesus' feet, thanking him for what he had done.*

A thankful heart grows your faith as you recognize God's work in your life.

1 CORINTHIANS 15:57 | *Thank God! He gives us victory over sin and death through our Lord Jesus Christ.*

Thank God because he gives you victory over sin and death when you put your faith in Jesus Christ.

COLOSSIANS 4:2 | *Devote yourselves to prayer with an alert mind and a thankful heart.*

JAMES 5:16 | *The earnest prayer of a righteous person has great power and produces wonderful results.*

Thank God because he answers prayer. Thankfulness in prayer acknowledges that God did something specific for you and that you are giving him the credit.

1 TIMOTHY 4:4 | *Since everything God created is good, we should not reject any of it but receive it with thanks.*

Thank God for the goodness and beauty of creation.

HABAKKUK 3:17-19 | *Even though the fig trees have no blossoms, and there are no grapes on the vines; even though the olive crop fails, and the fields lie empty and barren; even though the flocks die in the fields, and the cattle barns are empty, yet I will rejoice in the LORD! I will be joyful in the God of my salvation! The Sovereign LORD is my strength!*

A spirit of gratitude and praise changes the way you look at life. Complaining connects you to your unhappiness— thankfulness and praise connect you to the source of real joy. When you make thanksgiving a regular part of your life, you stay focused on all God has done and continues to do for you. Expressing gratitude for God's help is a form of worship.

How can I express my thankfulness?

PSALM 147:7 | *Sing out your thanks to the LORD; sing praises to our God with a harp.*

COLOSSIANS 3:16 | *Sing psalms and hymns and spiritual songs to God with thankful hearts.*

With music and singing.

PSALM 116:17 | *I will offer you a sacrifice of thanksgiving.*

Through generous giving.

PSALM 119:7 | *As I learn your righteous regulations, I will thank you by living as I should!*

Through obedience and service.

COLOSSIANS 4:2 | *Devote yourselves to prayer with an alert mind and a thankful heart.*

Through prayer.

PSALM 9:1 | *I will praise you, LORD, with all my heart.*

PSALM 104:1 | *Let all that I am praise the LORD. O LORD my God, how great you are! You are robed with honor and majesty.*

By praising and honoring God.

1 CHRONICLES 16:8 | *Give thanks to the LORD and proclaim his greatness. Let the whole world know what he has done.*

By telling others what God has done in your life and inviting them into relationship with him.

When should I give thanks to the Lord?

PSALM 92:2 | *It is good to proclaim your unfailing love in the morning, your faithfulness in the evening.*

Every morning and evening.

LUKE 9:16 | *Jesus took the five loaves and two fish, looked up toward heaven, and blessed them.*

When you are about to eat.

1 THESSALONIANS 5:18 | *Be thankful in all circumstances, for this is God's will for you who belong to Christ Jesus.*

Constantly and consistently.

Promise from God 1 CHRONICLES 16:34 | *Give thanks to the LORD, for he is good! His faithful love endures forever.*

TIREDNESS

What do I have to watch out for when I'm tired?

GALATIANS 6:9 | *Let's not get tired of doing what is good. At just the right time we will reap a harvest of blessing if we don't give up.*

Being tired makes you more susceptible to discouragement, temptation, and sin and causes you to lose hope that things will change in the future.

PROVERBS 30:1-2 | *I am weary, O God; I am weary and worn out, O God. I am too stupid to be human, and I lack common sense.*

Being tired causes you to lose perspective. When you're weary is not a good time to try to make important decisions.

JOB 10:1 | *I am disgusted with my life. Let me complain freely. My bitter soul must complain.*

Being tired can cause you to say things you may later regret.

ECCLESIASTES 1:8 | *Everything is wearisome beyond description. No matter how much we see, we are never satisfied. No matter how much we hear, we are not content.*

Being tired can cause you to lose your vision and purpose.

PSALM 127:2 | *It is useless for you to work so hard from early morning until late at night . . . for God gives rest to his loved ones.*

Always being tired may mean you are trying to do too much. It may be God's way of telling you to slow down.

2 SAMUEL 17:1-2 | *Ahithophel urged Absalom, "Let me choose 12,000 men to start out after David tonight. I will catch up with him while he is weary and discouraged. He and his troops will panic, and everyone will run away. Then I will kill only the king."*

Weariness makes you vulnerable to your enemies. When your guard is down, it's easier for them to attack you.

Who can help me when I grow tired?

HABAKKUK 3:19 | *The Sovereign LORD is my strength! He makes me as surefooted as a deer, able to tread upon the heights.*

EPHESIANS 6:10 | *Be strong in the Lord and in his mighty power.*

When you are weary, tap into the Lord's power—it is not some fable or fairy tale, but real supernatural power from the One who created you and sustains you.

1 KINGS 19:5-8 | *As he was sleeping, an angel touched him and told him, "Get up and eat!" . . . So he ate and drank and lay down again. Then the angel of the LORD came again and touched him and said, "Get up and eat some more, or the journey ahead will be too much for you." So he got up and ate and drank, and the food gave him enough strength to travel.*

You can help yourself by taking good care of your body: Exercise, rest, and eat nutritious meals. These activities will help you overcome weariness. Poor nutrition or health habits invite burnout.

ISAIAH 40:29-31 | *He gives power to the weak and strength to the powerless. Even youths will become weak and tired, and young men will fall in exhaustion. But those who trust in the LORD will find new strength. They will soar high on wings like eagles. They will run and not grow weary. They will walk and not faint.*

The Lord will give you renewed strength when you grow weary. When you come to him in praise, he refreshes your heart. When you come to him in prayer, he refreshes your soul. When you come to him in solitude, he refreshes your body. When you come to him in need, he refreshes your spirit. When you come to him with thankfulness, he refreshes your perspective. Coming to God releases the burdens of life and draws strength from him, the source of strength.

Promise from God MATTHEW 11:28 | *Jesus said, "Come to me, all of you who are weary and carry heavy burdens, and I will give you rest."*

TRUST

What does it mean to trust God?

PSALM 33:21 | *In him our hearts rejoice, for we trust in his holy name.*

REVELATION 4:11 | *You are worthy, O Lord our God, to receive glory and honor and power. For you created all things.*

Trusting God means recognizing that he is worthy of your trust and praise.

EPHESIANS 3:17 | *Christ will make his home in your hearts as you trust in him. Your roots will grow down into God's love and keep you strong.*

HEBREWS 3:14 | *If we are faithful to the end, trusting God just as firmly as when we first believed, we will share in all that belongs to Christ.*

Trusting God is an ongoing process based on a personal relationship with him.

GENESIS 6:13-14, 17, 22 | *God said to Noah, . . . "Build a large boat. . . . I am about to cover the earth with a flood." . . . Noah did everything exactly as God had commanded him.*

Trusting God means obeying his commands even when you don't fully understand why.

ROMANS 3:22 | *We are made right with God by placing our faith in Jesus Christ. And this is true for everyone who believes, no matter who we are.*

Trusting God means depending on Jesus Christ alone for salvation.

1 PETER 1:8 | *Though you do not see him now, you trust him; and you rejoice with a glorious, inexpressible joy.*

Trusting God means being confident in him even though you can't see him.

PROVERBS 3:5-7 | *Trust in the LORD with all your heart; do not depend on your own understanding. Seek his will in all you do, and he will show you which path to take. Don't be impressed* *with your own wisdom. Instead, fear the L*ORD *and turn away from evil.*

DANIEL 2:20-21 | *Praise the name of God forever and ever, for he has all wisdom and power. He controls the course of world events; he removes kings and sets up other kings.*

LUKE 1:38 | *Mary responded, "I am the Lord's servant. May everything you have said about me come true." And then the angel left her.*

Trusting God is acknowledging that he knows what is best, that he has everything under control, and that you surrender to his plan.

Why is trust a key in strong relationships?

LEVITICUS 6:2-4 | *Suppose one of you sins against your associate and is unfaithful to the L*ORD. *Suppose you cheat . . . or you steal or commit fraud, . . . [then] you are guilty.*

PROVERBS 20:23 | *The L*ORD *detests double standards; he is not pleased by dishonest scales.*

PROVERBS 25:19 | *Putting confidence in an unreliable person in times of trouble is like chewing with a broken tooth or walking on a lame foot.*

Mutual trust with family members or friends strengthens and deepens relationships because you know that what they tell you is true and that they are always acting in your best interests out of love. You have total peace of mind about them—you are free to fully enjoy those relationships. Mistrust is unhealthy and painful in relationships because it causes you to constantly question the motives of others.

Promise from God ISAIAH 26:3 | *You will keep in perfect peace all who trust in you, all whose thoughts are fixed on you!*

TRUTH

How does truth impact my relationship with God?

TITUS 1:2 | *[The] truth gives [those whom God has chosen] confidence that they have eternal life, which God—who does not lie—promised them before the world began.*

You can trust God because he always tells the truth. Nothing he has said in his Word, the Bible, has ever been proven wrong or false. He specifically created you in order to have a relationship with you for all eternity. If God says he loves you—and he always tells the truth—you can be sure he desires a relationship with you.

ISAIAH 33:15-16 | *Those who are honest and fair, who refuse to profit by fraud, who stay far away from bribes, . . . who shut their eyes to all enticement to do wrong—these are the ones who will dwell on high.*

Striving for honesty will help you experience the benefits of God's ultimate justice and protection.

JOHN 14:6 | *Jesus [said], "I am the way, the truth, and the life. No one can come to the Father except through me."*

ROMANS 1:18 | *God shows his anger from heaven against all sinful, wicked people who suppress the truth by their wickedness.*

God wants you to accept the ultimate truth that only by following Jesus can you spend eternity with him. He wants to spare you from the terrible consequences of pushing this most important truth away.

Does God really expect me to tell the truth all the time?

EXODUS 20:16 | *You must not testify falsely against your neighbor.*

PROVERBS 6:16-17 | *There are six things the LORD hates—no, seven things he detests . . . a lying tongue . . .*

God's law clearly forbids intentional lying.

EPHESIANS 4:15 | *We will speak the truth in love.*

Followers of Jesus are called to speak the truth, always in a loving manner.

Why is telling the truth so important?

PROVERBS 12:19 | *Truthful words stand the test of time, but lies are soon exposed.*

LUKE 16:10 | *If you are faithful in little things, you will be faithful in large ones. But if you are dishonest in little things, you won't be honest with greater responsibilities.*

Telling the truth is the litmus test to see if you are trying to model your life after the God of truth. If you are truthful in even small matters, you will have the reputation of being an honest person.

EPHESIANS 4:25 | *Stop telling lies. Let us tell our neighbors the truth, for we are all parts of the same body.*

Telling the truth promotes good relationships.

MATTHEW 12:33 | *A tree is identified by its fruit. If a tree is good, its fruit will be good. If a tree is bad, its fruit will be bad.*

Honest dealings reveal an honest character. What you do reveals who you are.

PSALM 24:3-5 | *Who may climb the mountain of the LORD? Who may stand in his holy place? Only those whose hands and hearts are pure, who . . . never tell lies. They will receive the LORD's blessing and have a right relationship with God their savior.*

Telling the truth is necessary for a relationship with God.

ROMANS 12:3 | *Be honest in your evaluation of yourselves, measuring yourselves by the faith God has given us.*

Honestly evaluating your walk with the Lord allows you to continue growing in your faith.

1 TIMOTHY 1:19 | *Cling to your faith in Christ, and keep your conscience clear. For some people have deliberately violated their consciences; as a result, their faith has been shipwrecked.*

Always telling the truth keeps a clear conscience.

PROVERBS 11:3 | *Honesty guides good people; dishonesty destroys treacherous people.*

There is freedom in honesty because you never have to worry about getting tripped up. Dishonesty and deception are a form of bondage because you get trapped by your lies.

Promise from God   PSALM 119:160 | *The very essence of your words is truth; all your just regulations will stand forever.*

UNITY

What is true unity?

ROMANS 12:4-5 | *Just as our bodies have many parts and each part has a special function, so it is with Christ's body. We are many parts of one body, and we all belong to each other.*

Unity is not the same as uniformity. Everyone has unique gifts and personalities. True unity is the celebration and appreciation of these differences to reach the common goal of serving God.

Why is unity important?

1 CORINTHIANS 1:10 | *I appeal to you, dear brothers and sisters, by the authority of our Lord Jesus Christ, to live in harmony with each other. Let there be no divisions in the church. Rather, be of one mind, united in thought and purpose.*

Unity allows you to share a sense of fellowship and devotion and to work together with a common purpose.

How can I help achieve unity?

ROMANS 15:5 | *May God, who gives this patience and encouragement, help you live in complete harmony with each other, as is fitting for followers of Christ Jesus.*

By working hard to develop the same kind of attitude Jesus had, one of patience and encouragement, of uniting not dividing.

EPHESIANS 4:12-13 | *Equip God's people to do his work and build up the church, the body of Christ. This will continue until we all come to such unity in our faith and knowledge of God's Son that we will be mature in the Lord, measuring up to the full and complete standard of Christ.*

By exercising your God-given responsibility to build others up.

1 PETER 3:8 | *All of you should be of one mind. Sympathize with each other. Love each other as brothers and sisters. Be tenderhearted, and keep a humble attitude.*

By sympathizing with others.

EPHESIANS 4:2-3 | *Always be humble and gentle. Be patient with each other, making allowance for each other's faults because of your love. Make every effort to keep yourselves united in the Spirit, binding yourselves together with peace.*

By being humble and gentle.

COLOSSIANS 3:13-14 | *Make allowance for each other's faults, and forgive anyone who offends you. Remember, the Lord forgave you, so you must forgive others. Above all, clothe yourselves with love, which binds us all together in perfect harmony.*

By loving and forgiving others.

Does unity mean everyone has to agree?

1 CORINTHIANS 12:12, 18-21 | *The human body has many parts, but the many parts make up one whole body. So it is with the body of Christ . . . and God has put each part just where he wants it. How strange a body would be if it had only one part! Yes, there are many parts, but only one body. The eye can never say to the*

hand, "I don't need you." The head can't say to the feet, "I don't need you."

Unity does not mean that everyone's opinion has to be the same, or even that their goals are the same. God has created everyone different, which means there will be differences of opinion. But your common purpose should be the same—to serve and honor God. Unity is ruined when selfish interests take priority over godly interests.

PSALM 34:14 | *Search for peace, and work to maintain it.*

EPHESIANS 4:11-13, 15-16 | *These are the gifts Christ gave to the church . . . to equip God's people to do his work and build up the church, the body of Christ. This will continue until we all come to such unity in our faith and knowledge of God's Son that we will be mature in the Lord. . . . We will speak the truth in love, growing in every way more and more like Christ. . . . He makes the whole body fit together perfectly. As each part does its own special work, it helps the other parts grow, so that the whole body is healthy and growing and full of love.*

Living peaceably with others does not mean avoiding conflict; it means handling conflict appropriately. Conflict handled poorly leads to fractured relationships. Avoiding conflict altogether leads to the same end because there is unresolved hurt or anger. Rather, when conflict arises, don't retaliate in anger but respond with love, relying on the Holy Spirit to give you the kind of patient endurance that leads to the resolution of the problem.

Promise from God GALATIANS 3:26-28 | *You are all children of God through faith in Christ Jesus. And all who have been* *united with Christ in baptism have put on Christ, like putting on new clothes. There is no longer Jew or Gentile, slave or free, male and female. For you are all one in Christ Jesus.*

WILL OF GOD

Does God really have a plan for my life?

PHILIPPIANS 1:6 | *I am certain that God, who began the good work within you, will continue his work until it is finally finished on the day when Christ Jesus returns.*

God has a plan for your life. The Bible talks about both a general plan and a specific plan for you. It is not an unthinking, automated script that you must follow. It is a journey with various important destinations and appointments, but also with a great deal of freedom as to the pace and scope of the travel.

PSALM 32:8 | *The LORD says, "I will guide you along the best pathway for your life. I will advise you and watch over you."*

God definitely wants to help you follow the path that will be most pleasing to him, and in the long run, it will be the most fulfilling to you, too. He wants you to follow a certain path toward his desired purpose for you, but he also cares about the details along the way. In both the big and small picture, God shows his love and care.

ESTHER 4:14 | *[Mordecai asked Esther,] "Who knows if perhaps you were made queen for just such a time as this?"*

JEREMIAH 29:11 | *"I know the plans I have for you," says the LORD. "They are plans for good and not for disaster, to give you a future and a hope."*

Sometimes you might be tempted to question God's will for your life, thinking he has made a mistake. Ultimately, what looks like a mistake to you now will be God's means to bring about something fulfilling and wonderful.

What are some things I should do to discover God's will for my life?

ROMANS 12:1-2 | *Give your bodies to God because of all he has done for you. Let them be a living and holy sacrifice—the kind he will find acceptable. . . . Don't copy the behavior and customs of this world, but let God transform you into a new person by changing the way you think. Then you will learn to know God's will for you, which is good and pleasing and perfect.*

Knowing God's will begins with knowing God. He holds nothing good back from you when you hold nothing back from him. As he transforms you into a new person, you come to understand his ways and enjoy living out his purpose for your life.

GENESIS 12:1, 4 | *The LORD had said to Abram, "Leave your native country, your relatives, and your father's family, and go to the land that I will show you." . . . So Abram departed as the LORD had instructed.*

To know God's will, you must obey God's Word.

ISAIAH 2:3 | *Come, let us go up to the mountain of the LORD. . . . There he will teach us his ways, and we will walk in his paths.*

JAMES 1:5 | *If you need wisdom, ask our generous God, and he will give it to you. He will not rebuke you for asking.*

1 JOHN 5:14 | *We are confident that he hears us whenever we ask for anything that pleases him.*

You can't sit around waiting for God to reveal his will for you; you must proactively look for it. Actively seek God's will through prayer, the Bible, conversation with mature believers and reliable advisers, and discernment of the circumstances around you.

ACTS 21:14 | *When it was clear that we couldn't persuade him, we gave up and said, "The Lord's will be done."*

Sometimes God's will for you becomes evident through circumstances beyond your control. You do the seeking, but you allow God to work out his will in the way he deems best. You will discover that you like where he takes you.

MATTHEW 25:21 | *Well done, my good and faithful servant. You have been faithful in handling this small amount, so now I will give you many more responsibilities.*

MATTHEW 25:29 | *To those who use well what they are given, even more will be given, and they will have an abundance.*

The natural abilities you have are gifts from God, and they are often a clue to what God wants you to do. Use whatever gifts you have been given to bring honor and glory to God, and you will be right where you need to be to discover God's will for you.

What are some of the things I can know are God's will for me?

PROVERBS 16:3 | *Commit your actions to the LORD, and your plans will succeed.*

God's will is that you do everything as if you were doing it for him. God has not revealed everything to his followers, but he has revealed all you need to know to live for him now.

AMOS 5:24 | *[The Lord says,] "I want to see a mighty flood of justice, an endless river of righteous living."*

God's will is that you seek justice at all times and do what is right.

1 CORINTHIANS 14:1 | *Let love be your highest goal!*

God's will is that you always love others.

MARK 10:45 | *Even the Son of Man came not to be served but to serve others and to give his life as a ransom for many.*

God's will is that you serve others, putting them above yourself.

EXODUS 20:1 | *God gave the people [a list of] instructions. . . .*

God's will is that you obey his laws for living.

GALATIANS 5:22-23, 25 | *The Holy Spirit produces this kind of fruit in our lives: love, joy, peace, patience, kindness, goodness, faithfulness, gentleness, and self-control. . . . Since we are living by the Spirit, let us follow the Spirit's leading in every part of our lives.*

God's will is that you live under the power and guidance of the Holy Spirit.

JAMES 4:17 | *Remember, it is sin to know what you ought to do and then not do it.*

When you are faced with the unknown, keep doing what you know to do: Love others, worship God, cultivate the work of the Holy Spirit in your life. Trust God to show you the next step when you need it.

Promise from God JEREMIAH 29:11 | *"I know the plans I have for you," says the LORD. "They are plans for good and not for disaster, to give you a future and a hope."*

WISDOM

How will having wisdom help me?

ROMANS 12:2 | *Don't copy the behavior and customs of this world, but let God transform you into a new person by changing the way you think. Then you will learn to know God's will for you, which is good and pleasing and perfect.*

2 CORINTHIANS 10:4-5 | *We use God's mighty weapons, not worldly weapons, to knock down the strongholds of human reasoning and to destroy false arguments. We destroy every proud obstacle that keeps people from knowing God. We capture their rebellious thoughts and teach them to obey Christ.*

Wisdom transforms head knowledge into action based on common sense. Wisdom from God helps you develop a biblical outlook that penetrates the deceptive and distorted thoughts of the world.

PSALM 111:10 | *Fear of the LORD is the foundation of true wisdom. All who obey his commandments will grow in wisdom.*

PROVERBS 9:10 | *Knowledge of the Holy One results in good judgment.*

Wisdom is not simply knowing facts and figures; it is also understanding the filter through which those facts and figures should be used. Wisdom recognizes that an all-powerful, all-knowing God has designed a moral universe with consequences for good or sinful choices. Wisdom begins with understanding your accountability to and your full dependence on your Creator. It's not *what* you know, but *whom* you know.

How do I obtain wisdom?

JOB 28:12, 21 | *Do people know where to find wisdom? Where can they find understanding? . . . It is hidden from the eyes of all humanity.*

PROVERBS 9:10 | *Fear of the LORD is the foundation of wisdom. Knowledge of the Holy One results in good judgment.*

Wisdom is elusive unless you actively pursue it. When you know God, you know where to find it.

PSALM 5:8 | *Lead me in the right path, O LORD. . . . Make your way plain for me to follow.*

JAMES 1:5 | *If you need wisdom, ask our generous God, and he will give it to you. He will not rebuke you for asking.*

God promises to give wisdom to anyone who asks. You need not be embarrassed to ask God for the wisdom and direction you need.

DEUTERONOMY 4:6 | *Obey [these decrees and regulations] completely, and you will display your wisdom and intelligence among the surrounding nations.*

PSALM 19:7 | *The instructions of the LORD are perfect, reviving the soul. The decrees of the LORD are trustworthy, making wise the simple.*

Obedience to God's Word—his commands, instructions, and teachings—will make you wise. The Bible is your most reliable source of wisdom and insight because it is the very counsel of God himself and therefore speaks to all situations.

1 CORINTHIANS 2:15-16 | *Those who are spiritual can evaluate all things, but they themselves cannot be evaluated by others. For, "Who can know the LORD's thoughts? Who knows enough to teach him?" But we understand these things, for we have the mind of Christ.*

Wisdom comes from the Holy Spirit, who lives in you when you believe in Jesus Christ.

PSALM 25:8-9 | *The LORD . . . leads the humble in doing right, teaching them his way.*

Wisdom comes more easily when you are humble.

PROVERBS 20:18 | *Plans succeed through good counsel.*

Wisdom often comes to you through the counsel of thoughtful, godly people.

Promise from God PROVERBS 1:23 | *Come and listen to my counsel. I'll share my heart with you and make you wise.*

WORK

→●

How should I view work?

GENESIS 1:27-28 | *God created human beings in his own image. . . .*
Then God blessed them and said, "Be fruitful and multiply. Fill
the earth and govern it. Reign over the fish in the sea, the birds in
the sky, and all the animals that scurry along the ground."

Know that there is value and honor in work. God created
people and gave them dominion over his creation. In other
words, God created you for work. Even before the Curse,
humanity was given the opportunity to transform the raw
materials of earth into things that would enhance life. Work
has always been meant to honor the Lord, to give people the
dignity of having something important to do, and to bring
blessings to others.

1 THESSALONIANS 4:11-12 | *Make it your goal to live a quiet life,*
minding your own business and working with your hands,
just as we instructed you before. Then people who are not
Christians will respect the way you live, and you will not need
to depend on others.

Your attitude toward work should include the goal of honoring God by the way you work, as well as supporting yourself
and others.

PROVERBS 13:11 | *Wealth from get-rich-quick schemes quickly*
disappears; wealth from hard work grows over time.

Honest, hard work is much better than schemes to get rich
quickly.

COLOSSIANS 3:17 | *Whatever you do or say, do it as a representative of the Lord Jesus, giving thanks through him to God the Father.*

Your goal is to work in such a way that you are a good representative of Jesus.

What if my work has nothing to do with anything "Christian"—how can God be glorified in my work?

GENESIS 2:2 | *On the seventh day God had finished his work of creation, so he rested from all his work.*

GENESIS 2:15 | *The LORD God placed the man in the Garden of Eden to tend and watch over it.*

2 THESSALONIANS 3:8 | *We worked hard day and night so we would not be a burden to any of you.*

Work is anchored in God's very character. Part of being made in God's image is sharing in the industrious and creative aspects of his nature. Gardening was the very first job given to humans. Christians are needed in all kinds of vocations. Whatever your job, believe that God has placed you there for a reason, and then do your work well as a service to him and as a way to serve others.

COLOSSIANS 3:23 | *Work willingly at whatever you do, as though you were working for the Lord rather than for people.*

The way you approach work is evidence of your relationship to Christ.

Can I work too hard?

PSALM 39:6 | *All our busy rushing ends in nothing.*

ECCLESIASTES 5:3 | *Too much activity gives you restless dreams.*

While you are called to work hard, make sure that your work doesn't so preoccupy you that you endanger your health, your relationships, or your time with God.

ACTS 16:16 | *She was a fortune-teller who earned a lot of money for her masters.*

Don't allow your work to compromise your values.

EXODUS 16:23 | *This is what the LORD commanded: Tomorrow will be a day of complete rest, a holy Sabbath day set apart for the LORD.*

MARK 6:31 | *Jesus said, "Let's go off by ourselves to a quiet place and rest awhile."*

There is a time to stop your work in order to rest, to celebrate life, and to worship God.

Is it possible to work your way into heaven?

EPHESIANS 2:9 | *Salvation is not a reward for the good things we have done.*

All our work and good deeds, no matter how impressive, will never save us.

Promise from God PHILIPPIANS 1:6 | *God, who began the good work within you, will continue his work until it is finally finished on the day when Christ Jesus returns.*

WORRY

When does worry become sin?

MATTHEW 13:22 | *The seed that fell among the thorns represents those who hear God's word, but all too quickly the message is crowded out by the worries of this life . . . so no fruit is produced.*

COLOSSIANS 3:2 | *Think about the things of heaven, not the things of earth.*

Worry is like thorny weeds—left uncontrolled, it crowds out what is good. Worry over the concerns of life becomes sin when it prevents the Word of God from taking root in your life.

How can I worry less?

PSALM 55:4-5 | *My heart pounds in my chest. . . . Fear and trembling overwhelm me, and I can't stop shaking.*

Worry and fear are normal responses to threatening situations, but often we imagine far worse scenarios than ever happen. Most of your worries never come true.

PSALM 62:6 | *[God] alone is my rock and my salvation, my fortress where I will not be shaken.*

Remembering that God's love and care for you are as solid as a rock can help keep your worries in perspective. He has everything under control.

MATTHEW 6:27 | *Can all your worries add a single moment to your life?*

Instead of adding more time or a better quality of life, worry diminishes your health and kills your joy.

PHILIPPIANS 4:6 | *Don't worry about anything; instead, pray about everything.*

1 PETER 5:7 | *Give all your worries and cares to God, for he cares about you.*

Talk to God openly about your worries. Hand them off to him as if to a consultant you totally trust or a supervisor you have the utmost confidence in.

PHILIPPIANS 4:8-9 | *Fix your thoughts on what is true, and honorable, and right, and pure, and lovely, and admirable. Think about things that are excellent and worthy of praise. . . . Then the God of peace will be with you.*

COLOSSIANS 3:2 | *Think about the things of heaven, not the things of earth.*

Fix your thoughts on the power of God, not the problems of life. Worry will always change you for the worse; God has the power to change you and your circumstances for the better. Turn your attention away from negative, unbelieving thoughts to the positive, constructive thoughts of faith and hope.

EXODUS 14:13 | *Don't be afraid. Just stand still and watch the LORD rescue you today.*

Combat worry and anxiety by remembering and trusting what God, in his Word, has already promised to do for you.

JOHN 14:1-3 | *Don't let your hearts be troubled. Trust in God, and trust also in me. There is more than enough room in my Father's home. If this were not so, would I have told you that I am going to prepare a place for you? When everything is ready,*

I will come and get you, so that you will always be with me where I am.

If you had ten million dollars in the bank, you wouldn't worry about providing for your family if you lost your job. In the same way, you know that God has provided for your future by preparing a perfect place for you in heaven. Let that assurance keep you from panicking in today's storms. The outcome is certain.

Promise from God   1 PETER 5:7 | *Give all your worries and cares to God, for he cares about you.*

WORTH

Am I really important to God?

GENESIS 1:26-27 | *God said, "Let us make human beings in our image, to be like us. They will reign over the fish in the sea, the birds in the sky, the livestock, all the wild animals on the earth, and the small animals that scurry along the ground." So God created human beings in his own image.*

PSALM 8:3-6 | *When I look at the night sky and see the work of your fingers . . . what are mere mortals that you should think about them . . . ? Yet you made them only a little lower than God and crowned them with glory and honor. You gave them charge of everything you made, putting all things under their authority.*

EPHESIANS 2:10 | *We are God's masterpiece. He has created us anew in Christ Jesus, so we can do the good things he planned for us long ago.*

God made you in his own image—you are his treasure and masterpiece! You are invaluable to him, which is why he sent his own Son to die for your sins so that you could live in heaven with him forever.

PSALM 139:13 | *You made all the delicate, inner parts of my body and knit me together in my mother's womb.*

JEREMIAH 1:5 | *[The Lord said,] "I knew you before I formed you in your mother's womb. Before you were born I set you apart and appointed you as my prophet to the nations."*

God made you with great skill and crafted you with loving care. He showed how much value he places on you by the way he made you.

PSALM 139:17 | *How precious are your thoughts about me, O God. They cannot be numbered!*

Almighty God thinks wonderful thoughts about you all the time. He looks inside you and sees your real value.

PSALM 139:1-3 | *O LORD, you have examined my heart and know everything about me. You know when I sit down or stand up. You know my thoughts even when I'm far away. You see me when I travel and when I rest at home. You know everything I do.*

God values you so much that he watches over you no matter where you are or what you are doing. This tells you how special he thinks you are.

1 CORINTHIANS 6:19-20 | *Don't you realize that your body is the temple of the Holy Spirit, who lives in you and was given to you by God? You do not belong to yourself, for God bought you with a high price.*

God values you so much that he even allows your body to become the temple in which he lives. God does not need to live in you. He can live anywhere. But by choosing to live within you, he declares you his temple, his dwelling place. What a great value he places on you to do that!

GALATIANS 3:26 | *You are all children of God through faith in Christ Jesus.*

GALATIANS 4:7 | *You are no longer a slave but God's own child. And since you are his child, God has made you his heir.*

God values you so much that he thinks of you as his child.

MATTHEW 28:20 | *[Jesus said,] "Be sure of this: I am with you always, even to the end of the age."*

God's Son promises to be with you always. Why would he want to be with you if he didn't value you?

Promise from God EPHESIANS 2:10 | *We are God's masterpiece. He has created us anew in Christ Jesus, so we can do the good things he planned for us long ago.*